A Long Day at the End of the World

A Long Day at the End of the World

Brent Hendricks

FARRAR, STRAUS AND GIROUX

NEW YORK

Farrar, Straus and Giroux
18 West 18th Street, New York 10011

Grateful acknowledgment is made for permission to reprint lyrics from "Personal Jesus," words and music by Martin Gore © 1989 Grabbing Hands Music Ltd. All rights in the U.S. and Canada controlled and administered by EMI Blackwood Music Inc. All rights reserved. International Copyright Secured. Used by Permission. Reprinted by Permission of Hal Leonard Corporation.

Library of Congress Cataloging-in-Publication Data
Hendricks, Brent R., 1958–
    A long day at the end of the world / Brent Hendricks. — 1st ed.
      p.   cm
    ISBN 978-0-374-14686-3 (pbk. : alk. paper)
    1. Hendricks, Brent, 1958—Family.   2. Authors, American—
21st century—Family relationships.   3. Crematoriums—Georgia.
4. Death care industry—Corrupt practices—Georgia.   I. Title

PS3608.E529Z46 2013
813'.6—dc23

                                                    2012028923

Designed by Abby Kagan

www.fsgbooks.com
www.twitter.com/fsgbooks • www.facebook.com/fsgbooks

1   3   5   7   9   10   8   6   4   2

For Kay and Kim,
who knew him well,

and for Kate and Xia,
who know him from pictures

And whosoever was not found written in the book of life was cast into the lake of fire.

—REVELATION 20:15

A Long Day
at the End
of the World

Because a picture is a sort of dream, the big moon circles the whirling earth that follows our little burning star, and my father hasn't entered the third state. He's not stretched out here in the backwoods of nowhere, becoming the ground. All the stars are flying away, the universe emptying out, my father emptied by the moon's glare until he's all shadow and light, beautiful almost, so overexposed he could be a young man in a photograph.

Light-seconds above, orbiting Hubble aims its lens—always backward into the night that was. Clicks a portrait of the artist as a young bomb.

We measure the future by measuring the past.

So where did he go? Where did the light go that was his body, the blood that cycled his veins, the too-bright picture of him with his sweetheart (my mother in her saddle oxfords and he in his jeans), their white shirts fused into the stone of an Oklahoma high school? Six years later he'd be flying out of a SAC base in Topeka, up to the North Pole and back, heavy with a single bomb.

And the other things: I know he dreamed of a wife and two kids, of a tall house inside the spiraling cloud of Georgia suburbs. I know he dreamed of moon travel, weekends, and the art of amateur photography. What about the pictures never taken of his sunken farm and flooded fields? And where did the light go that was his last smile as he slept and shivered in the empty air?

We've seen the end, having dreamed it—a cosmological sadness leaving no one left to measure the last gesture of the last thinking subject when the lights go out in the stars.

He lies in state. I consider this. And now somewhere in the far pines a mockingbird splits a strange tune—maybe Charlie Parker edged into Bob Wills—and it's 1954 all over again: my father on leave and fallen three sheets to the wind, lying in his new suit under a hurtling sky.

Just beyond, and in all known directions, the animals move upon the earth at night.

Part One

Part One

1

~~

I SNAPPED OFF THE CARDBOARD BACK of the wooden triangle and took it out. A slight musty smell rose from my hands, filled as they were with a thing that had been locked up for several years now. Dusty stars clung to my fingers while lines of color tumbled across the floor. Maybe you started with the stripes, I thought, kneeling down inside the four corners. Maybe it was mostly luck—luck and accumulation—like folding a map. Even halfway through I felt lucky, turning a quick corner into three points like a child making paper triangles. But reaching the end, I saw the same old picture again: my last rows twisted and dangling beneath a field of stars.

I wondered if I should try once more. Wasn't it a matter of simple geometry—easy crease and tuck like the soldiers did on TV? Yet I had failed every time I had tried to fold it. Over and over, I'd felt compelled to correct the improperly shaped thing in its cheap display case, and over and over, my efforts had come to bad ends.

So I stuffed Old Glory back into its container, blue patch of stars jutting out unevenly against crooked stripes. I hoped the neighbors wouldn't notice the flag case tucked beneath my arm, because I'd have to explain it. I'd have to say I was taking it—my father's burial flag—on a little trip, that I was going to carry it with me through the back roads of Alabama on a kind of pilgrimage.

And of course I couldn't stop there—on the loaded word "pilgrimage"—because they'd only want more. I'd have to say I was setting out on a trip through the low hills of northern Alabama, climbing Lookout Mountain, hoping to descend again into the valley: to the Tri-State Crematory in Noble, Georgia.

But my own bewilderment about the excursion itself, and about that flag, would prevent me from giving a practical description of what had happened at Tri-State. Instead, I'd probably head straight to the big trouble: I'd say, yes, astonishing as it may be, my father had died and his bones had been resurrected. And then those same bones, the bones of my father, had been abandoned at the Tri-State Crematory for five years. The man was dead, rose again, and dwelled among the other dead for a time.

Even in the South, such apocalyptic declarations might overwhelm my devout neighbors. But the story required no articles of faith. My father had died and I had gone to his funeral and he was buried in the ground. I saw him lowered into the red dirt. My father was dead and the doors of his grave flew open and he came again upon the earth.

I would have to tell all that to my neighbors because I didn't know what else to say. I was setting off to unholy ground, to a field with a lake where hundreds of bodies once lay scattered and alone, hoping that something would happen. For a while I'd lived with an image of my father lying lost at the Tri-State Crematory, and I needed to change it. I needed to take a ride to Tri-State and see where he'd lain those long years. I needed to tell him goodbye, or hello and goodbye, or tell him nothing but that I had tried. I had tried to make amends for his troubled bones.

And I had that flag, wrapped up all crooked and wrong, to prove it.

2

~~

THERE ARE FLOWERS that grow mostly in disturbed areas. In the middle of May, when I turned onto University Avenue in Tuscaloosa, I was thinking about those flowers. Passionflower and mistflower. Morning glory and fleabane. A copy of the *National Audubon Society Field Guide to the Southeastern States*, which I'd spent some time with the previous evening, pressed against my father's burial flag on the front seat. I was thinking about those flowers, and the idea of those flowers, as I rode through the old downtown.

To be honest, the phrase "disturbed areas" had always bothered me in my occasional searches regarding plant habitat—I really didn't know what it meant—and yet last night that ambiguity seemed suddenly strange, almost ominous. I could easily imagine the other landscapes offered by the field guide: "moist pinelands," "meadows," "thickets," even the more poetic "rich woods." And I could see the "ditches" and "roadsides" that some species favored. But the phrase "disturbed areas" was so abstract. If it didn't include marred ground such as "ditches"—if it meant something more—then I could envision only horribly dug-up places, unearthed and scarred.

I was considering this phrase, then, as I drove past the rubble of what was until recently the home of, respectively, Norris Radiator, Auto Trim & Tire, and the Firestone Tire and Service Center. I passed the old post office—set for destruction next—and gazed down Sixth Street, where soon the Diamond Theater would disappear forever, along with KSV restaurant (a soul-food buffet that doubled as the Orchid nightclub), and the longtime Tuscaloosa News Building. City planners had also scheduled demolition for various other businesses—two shoe-repair shops, a barbershop, a pool hall, a paint store, an antiques shop, and several furniture stores. Maybe the place would be better off in the end. I didn't know—it was okay the way it was. Yet there were no flowers springing from these ruins; this was not a disturbed area in the strict sense of the phrase.

On the other hand, I knew of at least one place that had to be a disturbed area, if that meant a natural location generally torn up by backhoe, a place where the earth was moved from here to there, trenches dug and the ground cleaved. Black-eyed Susan, Venus's looking glass, Queen Anne's lace, Carolina cranesbill, peppergrass, chickweed, fleabane, southern dewberry, blue toadflax, Asiatic dayflower, painted leaf, kudzu, poison ivy, prickly sow thistle, horrible thistle—at least some of those flowers must have flourished at the Tri-State Crematory, blooming among the dead.

I first learned about the Tri-State Crematory when I glanced up at the television to see emergency workers in north Georgia rummaging through the thick brush surrounding a rural area. At the time—February 2002—I was living in Portland, Oregon, and I distinctly remember a helicopter onscreen, beating overhead, filming the workers from above at night, the spotlight causing their green jackets to flicker on and off against dark trees. Apparently, the workers had uncovered a few dozen decomposed corpses sprawled about the crematory grounds. The news report explained there would be more bodies to come.

By Sunday morning, authorities had recovered ninety-five bodies from the Tri-State Crematory and feared that many more—hundreds, perhaps—lay scattered throughout the overgrown premises. There were accounts of bodies piled in pits, bodies in shacks, bodies stuffed into metal vaults beneath a small lake.

Eventually—after a series of Gothic events, blackly fantastic—the full extent of the desecration was revealed. In all, authorities recovered 339 decomposing bodies, making the Tri-State Crematory Incident the largest mass desecration in modern American history.

And the details of the incident were gruesome, to say

the least. More than thirty of the bodies were discovered in the main crematory building and two storage sheds, either lying on the floor or piled high in metal vaults. The remaining three-hundred-plus bodies were distributed throughout the dense brush and woods of the crematory grounds. Of this larger group, the majority were dumped into eight burial pits of varying depth, which were then covered with dirt, trash, and, in one instance, an old pool table. Body parts were found sticking out of the pits, like grisly plantings in a neglected garden.

The skeletal remains of other bodies were strewn haphazardly through the brush on cardboard and plywood burn pallets. Still others were discovered in discarded body bags beneath the pines. Finally, a small group still lay in their caskets (generally cremations do not involve the added expense of a casket), and the rats had found their way into those enclosures, shuffling the bones.

My father's bones were among those found at Tri-State, where he lay abandoned for five years. And for five years the crematory backhoe dug pits and built mounds, divided the earth and piled it up, opened the ground and closed it. The metal edge leveled trees and heavy brush, crushed kudzu and passionflower, chickweed and thistle. And in so doing made a new place for all these things to grow.

My mother, it seems, had her own idea about altering the ground.

On the third day of the Tri-State Crematory Incident—as the reports told of more bodies piled up in pits, more bodies scattered in the brush, possibly many more locked in metal vaults beneath the lake—I knew only that my father's corpse had been sent to a crematory in the area five years before.

On the far end of the phone I heard the same news account blare back at me from my mother's den in Santa Fe, the same helicopter hovering above. She didn't know if the body had been sent to Tri-State. But from her tone I could tell she felt particularly anxious about the potential bad news, though not only because her husband's corpse might be involved. There was more. Her anxiety arose from an event that occurred five years before Tri-State, which began with a phone call saying she was going to "dig Daddy up."

Such an odd phrase, heavy and hard. But at the time I immediately understood it—her burial phobia had gotten the best of her. In her haste and disorientation at my father's abrupt death, my mother had purchased two plots in the small cemetery of their north Georgia resort community. For seven years it appeared she had subsumed her long-standing fear of being buried, of "sleeping with worms," as she often said. Suddenly, however, in 1997, she announced she wanted to exhume my father, have him cremated and then shipped out to New Mexico. That way, she calmly stated, she could avoid the worms and have my father nearby. And when she died she would also be cremated, their ashes scattered together over the New Mexico mountains.

Did we—my sister and I—want to come to his exhumation party?

My sister, Kim, who lived in Houston, and I were stunned. We all knew my mother was eccentric, but all this talk about Daddy's *party* was a bit alarming. Yet after a flurry of conversations and e-mails we decided it was all my mother's show. If she wanted to go through with this bizarre idea, it was really her right to do so. We would not try to dissuade her, though we did not want to participate either. So it was that my father reentered this plane as a modern-day Lazarus, torn from the earth by a backhoe.

For my mother, this unburying proved helpful. She placed his remains in a black box that she kept in a special nook for family memorabilia. Now she was freed from her fate of worms and at the same time felt less alone in the world. In fact, she talked to the box throughout the day—sad though it may be—and her interaction with him was somehow therapeutic.

So when my mother spoke to me on that day in February 2002—before we knew that my father's body had been sent to the Tri-State Crematory—there was an edge to her voice. My God, had she dug up her husband for a psychological reason, to assuage her own burial phobia, only to facilitate his arrival at Tri-State? Had he been lying for five years in the woods, in a deep pit, in a stuffed vault sunk beneath that awful lake? Had she made some terrible mistake?

The first step, of course, was to find out whether my father had actually been sent to the Tri-State hell camp. That would take some phone calls over the next two days. In the meantime, *Honor thy mother* must have been ingrained in my brain because I didn't mention anything about the exhumation during our conversation. And, as she later explained, she got off the phone and didn't say a word to that black box—the one she'd talked to for five years—the box now filled with God knows what and God knows who.

The flag case kept sliding around on the front seat, and I pulled over and tried to buckle it in. The stars and rumpled stripes gave the effect of a slouched and harried traveler. So I asked if it was okay, if it was comfortable. Did it want the air conditioner on?

As it happened, I had pulled over in front of a historical marker: ALABAMA CORPS OF CADETS DEFENDS TUSCALOOSA. Like everyone who walked past the marker on occasion, I had read the thick print before, but today I decided to get out and study it more closely. This would be part of my ritual, I thought, the making of meaning as I traveled along. The official marker read like an encyclopedia entry, dispassionately describing the futile actions of a ragtag group of teenage boys who defended the city from the federal "enemy" during the Civil War—the word "enemy," I'm sure, being just a little slip of the engraver.

Behind me I could hear the rumble of heavy machinery clawing at a fresh pile of rubble where the new federal building would soon rise. And then something strange happened, something I'd like to attribute to the thunderous and timely collapse of another old building, yet I heard no calamity of such kind. I'd like to say I felt the sidewalk shift, a small swerve and tumble, right there at the center of the city. I'd like to say I didn't just falter over my worn-out boots, stumbling as I turned back toward the car.

We've all felt it at some point: a dizziness, an unexplained misstep, or perhaps in my case a little giddiness about my trip momentarily depriving my brain of oxygen. But this was ritual and magic, I told myself, look around.

And I saw an elderly black man, who did not look up, turn slowly into Oak City Barber & Beauty Shop: the only black barbershop downtown not scheduled for destruction. A simple image, without consequence, but as a matter of mission and belief something else entirely. As a matter of seeking and finding, of moving toward revelation, I wondered—in the miraculous sense of that word—if my small spot on earth, the ground where I stood, had trembled in the wake of the old man's passing.

3

~

I'D RETURNED TO THE SOUTH a couple of years earlier, when my wife took a job teaching creative writing at the University of Alabama. I had never been to Tuscaloosa. After much discussion we'd decided to try it out. I left my part-time law job in Northampton, Massachusetts; we packed up our old silver Saab with keepsake things, like my flag case, that we didn't trust to the moving truck; and sadly we waved goodbye to our beautiful 1840s mill house nestled in the foothills of the Berkshires.

Kate had never been to the South, having grown up in a liberal Jewish household in Boston, but I convinced her it would be okay. Surely, by now, the Deep South would be more charitable than the Atlanta suburbs I grew up in during the 1970s. Surely the tolerant winds of Atlanta proper, where I'd happily lived in midtown after law school, would have reached the western edge of Alabama. And besides, Tuscaloosa was a college town; I knew more than a few great college towns in the South—small cultural hot spots like Athens, Lafayette, and Charlottesville.

We were middle-aged hipsters, literary types. We'd led the bohemian life in Portland—before Portland was the youthful mecca it is now—frequenting blown-out clubs to hear our friends play music, haunting neighborhood bars, blathering away about Nietzsche in old diners. A little pretentious, maybe, but God was it fun. And finally a bit frazzled, tired of the rain, we left the West Coast to live the quieter life of western Mass.—to live in the country among trees and bears.

What did I expect from Tuscaloosa? Not much, really. Maybe a modest counterculture. Maybe a sustainable core of different-minded, broad-minded people. Maybe a couple of good coffee shops and a bookstore. Maybe a record store. At her job interview, one of Kate's future colleagues had reassured her that unlike what Gertrude Stein had said about another place ("there is no there there"), Tuscaloosa did have a there there.

But we never found it. If it actually existed, it was doing a damn fine job of hiding out. In fact, nearly everyone we knew at the University of Alabama—from creative writers, to artists, to scholars—wanted to get the hell out. Almost everyone, when the annual academic job listings appeared, scrambled to land a position elsewhere. True, a few friends in town had made their peace, and I don't mean to subtract from their lives. But to us it felt like nothing was going on, or what was going on was the opposite of what we had going on.

It was perplexing. It was as if the things you took for granted simply didn't exist: a decent movie theater, a library, a good public school for our four-year-old daughter. And though we felt alienated, sometimes desperately so, I came to believe that our liberal Christian friends had it worse—mostly Episcopalians who'd experienced viable religious communities in cities like Memphis, Nashville, and Atlanta. We joked that the Enlightenment just hadn't made it this far west down Interstate 59 from Birmingham— that Descartes was just some Cajun guy from Louisiana. A Catholic, no doubt.

In dark resignation—or simply to survive—we embraced the war cry of the Crimson Tide, the vaunted University of Alabama football team. *Roll Tide*, we'd all say for no particular reason. It became our salutation, acclamation, and glorification. It became our filler phrase and our phrase for goodbye.

—"Hey Abe, you want to have a beer on the porch?"

"Roll Tide, brother."

—"Kate, honey, I'm running out for more milk."

"Roll Tide."

—"Did you hear Michael got a story in *Esquire*?"

"Jesus Christ, Roll Tide!"

A form of resistance, really, a phrase that meant everything and nothing, a couple of words that helped us get by.

As I traveled over the Black Warrior River, I liked to picture Hernando de Soto crossing the same river several miles to the south in a makeshift boat—not only the clanking helmets, chain mail, and lances, but also the manacles of slaves and spiked collars of war dogs.

De Soto trooped through Georgia and Alabama in 1540, searching for gold. He left thousands of Native Americans dead on battlefields, with many more thousands lost to disease carried by his fellow explorers and an accompanying herd of European pigs. A man of customary conquistador habits, he tortured and mutilated his Indian captives for information and sport, enslaving both men and women as his army wandered through the countryside. And following his gory expedition, the conqueror left a large swath of land blighted and abandoned.

Though our goals were essentially different, we both traversed the river here for a specific reason. The fact is that Tuscaloosa lies on the fall line, the geological boundary at which the Piedmont and the Coastal Plain meet. In past ages the area below the fall line comprised a vast sea, with the Piedmont forming a rocky and hilly shoreline. As the sea receded, the sandy underwater floor emerged to create the modern Coastal Plain. Today—without human intervention in the form of locks and dams—Southern rivers above the fall line remain difficult to travel, while the deeper water below flows more smoothly to the ocean.

The practical effect of all this was that people tended to settle near the fall line. For de Soto it meant he found a Native settlement below that boundary in the lush land known as the meander zone, where the river slowed down and began to cut back upon itself, creating rich soil for farming and fertile backwater for fishing. He pillaged that town for corn and other necessities in late November 1540. Nearly three hundred years later, it meant that the first white settlers established a trading post (at the site of another soon-to-disappear Indian village) where they could ship deerskins and timber downstream to the port of Mobile. In time the city of Tuscaloosa came into being, and in time I had my bridge to cross over, gazing into the black water flowing smoothly in both directions.

De Soto was also relevant for other reasons. In his bloody wanderings the explorer passed near the present site of the Tri-State Crematory, moving southward from Tennessee. He buried his dead, including Indian slaves that may have been my ancestors, in a valley not too far from the crematory where my father's bones would later lie. And in leaving the ground around him disturbed, his gaze remained fixed on an absent thing—his dazzling piles of gold—just as I remained focused on the lost body of my father.

On the other side of the river, traveling north on Highway 69, I left Tuscaloosa and entered Northport—another small town within our tiny metropolitan area. Immediately I saw a glossy sign for the new Dreamland, one of several slick franchise offspring of the original dive barbecue joint still serving ribs up in the Tuscaloosa hills. On my left I could make out the roofs of Historic Northport, a beautiful block of ancient buildings that had been miraculously preserved and that now housed a range of expensive and down-home establishments. And ahead stretched a mile of dilapidated shopping centers and businesses—some with familiar names from the past (Piggly Wiggly) and others that remained poignantly anonymous (Desperado's Gifts and Collectibles, Claws and Paws, Bama Cash Express). The obligatory strip-mall churches (Grace Ministries, Living Faith Worship Center) also appeared, as well as a couple of stand-alone churches. Many of the storefronts lay empty, though a few new national banks had made their first inroads.

When I saw a Walgreens drugstore rise in the distance, signaling a shift in commercial and cultural development, I quickly pulled right onto a cross street in search of a local landmark—Archibald's—by legend the most old-time African American barbecue place around.

Ever since moving to town I'd heard about Archibald's, but no one, including the phone book, could give an exact address, and no one could provide proper directions except to say that it lay somewhere east of Highway 69, over the river. All previous expeditions had left me wandering and bewildered. Today the brick houses I passed gradually became poorer, leading to a housing project, and then, following a sequence of turns I could not describe to anyone, I stumbled upon the place.

A fire smoldered in a trash can and another, bigger fire blazed next to a broken shack. No indication it was a restaurant, except the smell of smoked pork that swept through my car and clothes. Satisfied and illuminated, I breathed it all in, as only an erstwhile vegetarian prone to backsliding might do. Here lay the real counterculture of Tuscaloosa County, the one white folks like me could only visit: a place for lunch—a cement shed with a few stools, languishing among the brush and vines of the floodplain.

4
~

ALL I HAD FOR A DESTINATION was a field in a picture, a bulldozed and flattened piece of land. After sifting through all those bodies, the pits and trash and heavy brush, after the long and sometimes failed process of identifying bodies—especially those piled high in the pits, whose flesh had been commingled and thus degraded—the authorities decided to raze the crematory grounds as a memorial to the desecration. It was agreed, among the parties involved, that the property would be allowed to return to its natural state, held in perpetuity as an undeveloped and wild place.

In the photograph, which I had pulled off the Internet, the field had just been plowed under, leaving thick tread marks in rough lines. A single white pine and a single oak stood front and left of center; more vague trees rimmed the edge, but the rest looked as flat and empty as the moon. I wondered whose father or mother or child lay between those two trees, moldering below the earth or festering in the air, and how long that body had lain there, changing with the seasons. Soon, of course, the flowers would come to this field (the photograph was about two years old) and then most likely tall grasses and more pines. But the first flowers would be of the disturbed variety— black-eyed Susan, Venus's looking glass, sweet everlasting— the flowers born of upheaval and big machines.

"In the eyes: dream . . ." begins Rainer Maria Rilke's poem describing his father in a faded old photograph. His father, with whom he had a tumultuous relationship, was a failed imperial officer in the Austrian military. My father was an amateur photographer who took pictures to keep track of things—to remember them—but mostly because he liked the machines. "O quickly disappearing photograph," ends Rilke's poem, "in my more slowly disappearing hand."

I said *look at this*, and weirdly my own face reflected off the clear plastic case, merging with rows of crooked stripes. I looked like my father: we had the same black eyes and flat smile, the same high cheekbones. I smiled into the blue field of stars and glanced away.

I said *look at this* because my father would have recognized the scene. He had dragged us to the new suburbs of Atlanta when I was twelve, in fact dragged us to a new home every two years because he worked for IBM. My older sister and I would shout "**I**'ve **B**een **M**oved" as we piled into the car for a new house, a new school, and a new set of friends. It was corporate policy, nationwide, meant to force promising white-collar employees to forge allegiance to the corporation and not to a place. It worked. We were the typical American family of a generation ago, dislocated and uprooted before any firm roots were put down. Tulsa, Oklahoma; Bartlesville, Oklahoma; Springfield, Missouri; Weston, Connecticut; and then Atlanta, Georgia. Each new home never really a home, and I was just going into the seventh grade.

The land in my north Atlanta suburb appeared always under siege. In every direction the dirt lay exposed and piled up, making way for new, mostly treeless subdivisions with rows of fake-colonial box houses, with an occasional garage fastened to a different end of the same regular box for variety. New highways built, old country roads widened, chain gangs (real chains linking a gang of black men in white convict clothes) doing most of the digging and widening, filling in of streams, and chopping up of rattlesnakes, copperheads, and cottonmouths with shiny pickaxes. Farms converted to town houses and country clubs blooming among the subdivisions, more trees leveled for the eighteen holes and the tennis courts and the swimming pools. And then to service this blossoming civilization, another line of new roads and chain gangs and shopping centers and churches.

On this day, I saw Queen Anne's lace lingering along the roadside, kudzu devouring a stand of pines. And I saw what I'd seen years ago in Atlanta: the earth gouged out for gas stations and apartment complexes, and for new subdivisions with oddly similar brick houses seemingly dropped from space onto flattened lots. Daisies struggled in ditches and loose ground alongside LAND FOR SALE signs suggesting more digging to come. And then, as in Atlanta, some modest brick houses appeared that must once have been country houses, and near these older houses a trailer park (spent frames rusting with vines and dirty toys in front) that would soon relocate farther out.

The most important feature of these developing neighborhoods lay hidden from view: the dead end. At my dead ends, often just cul-de-sacs surrounded by woods and half-finished houses, teenagers began arriving at twilight on their bikes. We'd sit on the backhoes and rustle through construction debris, careful to sidestep the poison ivy and pink briar. We'd stomp along subfloors and smoke cigarettes on the open stairs. We'd carry beers stolen from our parents' refrigerators and chug them in unpainted kitchens. We'd kiss awkwardly in doorways, boys and girls playing games in giant dollhouses.

After dark, the older teenagers took dominion. They (eventually including me) cruised through in Firebirds and Trans Ams, Volkswagens and Delta 88s, as word spread quickly about a newly carved-out cul-de-sac, a fresh breach in the thick pines and oaks. Always there was another dead end, in fact several of these oases—scaffolded and vacant, immune from adults and temporarily hidden from the law. Car radios blared in the night, generally pitting a gang in favor of Neil Young's "Southern Man," which chastised the South for its flagrant racism, against those who preferred Lynyrd Skynyrd's "Sweet Home Alabama," which chastised Neil Young for chastising the South and which praised the blatantly racist Alabama governor George Wallace. (The Lynyrd Skynyrd album cover, like many of the Southern state flags at the time, proudly pictured the Confederate Battle Flag, the square X also known as a St. Andrew's cross.) In general, the kids who'd Been Moved like myself fell into the Neil Young camp, while the native Southerners sided with the Confederates. For the most part, however, given our age and predicament, the political animosities never ran too deep and the groups pretty much got along. The New South was as strange to them as the Old South was to us. Thrown together in that altered suburban landscape, we shared a bewilderment that fostered camaraderie across cliques and politics.

In that hot Southern dark, the sweet smell of pot and honeysuckle collected around our asphalt circle. We'd laugh and goof off. Eventually a parent from a nearby box house would call the police and—with a sixth sense finely tuned from practice—we'd fly back into our cars, slipping away to another dead end on an endless circuit. And maybe later we'd roll back into those hidden places and park our cars, finding new ways to extend our fine new bodies and limbs. But that's it. That's all we had to do in our far-removed Atlanta suburb after cruising McDonald's and the Pizza Hut parking lot.

I think the corporate kids were disturbed the most. We'd come from Connecticut and Illinois and California—from suburbs, yes, but ones attached to large cities with established progressive cultures. Atlanta, at that time, had no real cultural identity that spoke to us, other than its historical role in the civil rights movement, which our white suburban schools emphatically downplayed. And anyway the city was so far away, nearly thirty miles, which prevented us from regularly enjoying, for example, the single block of counterculture that bubbled up in Little Five Points, a small outpost lying even farther south than Emory University. In its place we had Southern Pride, that Confederate flag. And we had the earth itself, always torn up and exposing its rich red clay and then grassed over into homogenous subdivisions.

I have a friend whom I see sometimes, my only friend I still know from that period, and we always have to talk about it: the zeros, the wind of nothingness that blew through our brains back then. The howl that ached to enter all of us and overtake us, propel us toward fraternities and sororities, and later whip us into corporate beings just like our parents.

Of course I blamed them for the whole thing, especially my father. I blamed him for the stress of moving every two years, for the new friends I had to make and then replace along the way, for hauling me into this particularly blank wind and leaving me there.

And probably my frustrated response to Tuscaloosa reflected my prior troubles—I harbored a simmering rage against my old suburb that I instinctively projected upon the present and that, in its quickness, tended to uncomplicate the forces at play. Even so, I believed a region *was* forged by the big plates underneath, the seismic shifts that allow for relatively stable or unstable ground.

And as for my father, he was just a man bound up in the lingerings of a certain time and place, whose connection to disturbance began much earlier, at his own beginnings upon our movable earth.

5

~~~

WHEN HERNANDO DE SOTO PLUNDERED the ancient valley that would later hold the Tri-State Crematory, he
searched for a legendary hoard of gold. It was one way—
the expensive way—to acquire that substance, involving
the building of ships, the outfitting of expeditions, and the
arming of soldiers to subdue Native populations. But back
in Europe, in quieter fashion, early scientists sought to
transmute base metals into gold. They attempted, through
research and experimentation, to discover the philoso-
pher's stone: the essential ingredient in transforming lead
into gold, and water into the fountain of youth. Spiritual
wisdom remained the ultimate goal of the alchemist,
with infinite wealth and infinite longevity as manifesta-
tions of that wisdom. Unfortunately for the alchemists—
as well as millions of indigenous people—marauding and
pillaging the New World proved more effective in produc-
ing gold.

Strangely, nearly five hundred years later, a man named

Brent Marsh practiced a different kind of alchemy at the Tri-State Crematory. In fact, he grew quite successful at it, and his particular branch of the science never failed to work.

During the first days of the discovery of the Tri-State Crematory Incident, the press—including *Newsweek*, *USA Today*, and the *Atlanta Journal-Constitution*—ran stories that registered the widespread community shock at the desecration. Over and over, Brent Marsh's friends, acquaintances, and business relations expressed the highest regard for his family and its individual members, making their collective fall from grace so precipitous.

In framing the history of the Marsh family, the *Atlanta Journal-Constitution* searched the genealogical records at the Walker County Library and discovered a potential white ancestor dating to the late 1700s. Not surprisingly, the connection remained murky. But without ambiguity, the Marsh bloodline did lead back to the first black child born in the county, Willie Marsh, around 1830. For nearly 170 years, then, the family lived as black citizens— second-rate citizens—in an overwhelmingly white part of Georgia.

Yet Brent Marsh's immediate predecessors did much to soften racial prejudice in the area. His mother, Clara Chestnut Marsh, taught school in Walker County for over thirty years. She also served as chairwoman of the local

Democratic Committee and in 1995 received the Walker County Woman of the Year Award from the Chamber of Commerce. Her greatest devotion, however, she reserved for the New Home Missionary Baptist Church, located down the road from the crematory property. Intimately involved with the congregation's functions, she sang in the choir each Sunday morning.

Her husband, Ray Marsh, started and ran two successful businesses: the Tri-State Crematory and Marsh Vault and Grave Service. Well liked and respected, he managed to acquire customers across racial lines, a strong achievement in this rural corner of the state. "Nobody, white or black, said anything negative against them," stated William J. Willis Jr., proprietor of a funeral home in Dalton, Georgia. And when Ray Marsh became bedridden due to a stroke, his son, Brent, took over the family business in 1996. The elder Marshes remained owners.

Brent was a big guy, six two and 265 pounds, a local high school football star who "was everybody's friend," according to Christy Anderson, a former classmate. "You couldn't ask for a nicer fellow." In 1992, he received a scholarship to nearby University of Tennessee at Chattanooga, where he played middle linebacker and majored in business. When his father fell ill, he left school and never completed his degree.

Some people speculated that Brent Marsh didn't want to step into his father's shoes, that his mother had pressured him, one of five children, to take over operation of the crematory. Eddie Upshaw, a longtime family friend, recalled that Brent "talked about teaching and coaching. But this was laid in his hand after his dad got sick. And he wasn't going to turn his back on his family." He did his duty. And within a year, at the age of twenty-four, he had abandoned and desecrated his first body.

During the next five years, Brent Marsh appeared remarkably normal in his everyday activities—including hosting his own wedding party on his family's private lake, the very lake on whose hidden shores lay scattered and decomposing bodies. He coached youth football and basketball, acted as deacon at the New Home Church, and even took his father's place on the board of the Walker County Division of Family and Children Services.

"He was just an ordinary guy," said Ray Newton, who delivered a load of dirt to the crematory during the desecration period. "Just the nicest guy you'd ever want to know."

To Mike Worthington, the co-owner of Smokey's B-B-Q, Marsh appeared to have it all: a successful business; a beautiful young wife; a new baby daughter, miraculously born on Super Bowl Sunday. Like any doting father, a regular guy, he carried photographs of the new arrival around in his wallet, which he'd recently shown off while dining at the restaurant.

"He loved hot wings," added Terri Worthington, Mike's wife and co-owner of the barbecue joint. "He was well-schooled, very articulate, well-spoken."

Yes, Marsh seemed to have done a real Jekyll and Hyde on his hometown and, after his arrest, performed a personal disappearing act. At every hearing he looked stone-faced and blank. He didn't react. He didn't smile. He appeared neither confused nor bewildered—only absent, vanished, more dead than alive. It was an expression that never changed during the long and very public ordeal of the Tri-State Crematory Incident.

On the Mr. Hyde side of things, back at the crematory, Marsh concocted an elaborate scheme of deception.

Typically, when a bereaved family chooses cremation through a local funeral home, the family expects to receive in exchange for a fee (and a corpse) the incinerated remains of the deceased person. This bodily residue—the cremains—consists entirely of bone fragments, which the crematory operator machine-grinds into a fine dust. Brent Marsh, however, had a big problem. He hadn't incinerated those 339 corpses in the first place. Yet he clearly needed something to return to the funeral home and ultimately the family—some substance that would pass as human cremains.

Marsh's solution to this problem was ingenious and bizarre. Having grown up assisting his father in the family business, he was familiar with the appearance and texture of proper cremains. He knew what he was looking for. After experimenting with various combinations and proportions, he settled on a special blend of ground bone and concrete dust that possessed the consistency of talcum powder. During the years of desecration, he gradually used less bone and more concrete dust in his mixture, finally substituting only the fake powder. Though slightly more fine than pulverized bone, the powder evidently offered a reasonable resemblance to true cremains. In fact, as a crude chemist—or in this case an alchemist attempting to transmute base materials into a sacred substance—he encountered no detractors. The family members who came across the hundreds of faked cremains, and every funeral home worker for that matter, fell for his strange sleight of hand.

Nevertheless, the time necessary to discover and perfect his process of transmutation, as well as the care he took to reproduce the results hundreds of times over, could simply have been used to cremate the corpses properly. Why not just incinerate all 999 bodies received from 1997 to 2002, rather than create this elaborate deception for 339 of them? Wasn't it actually more trouble to further this deceit than simply do the job as expected?

And with a fuel cost savings of only $175 per body, Marsh's legerdemain grossed about $10,000 a year on average—hardly worth the risk given the extremely high chance of eventual discovery. Even if he needed the money, one could stash only so many rotting bodies on the crematory grounds without the stench drifting too far on a hot summer day, or the bones glowing too clearly through the bare trees of winter.

So why? Why did he do it?

From the beginning, the vacant Brent Marsh offered no clues. That reality—coupled with a lack of strong motive—left only the evidence. What was clear was this: Chaos held dominion at the Tri-State Crematory.

When the authorities first entered the large storage shed, bodies lay scattered among refuse and, incredibly, Christmas decorations. Other corpses floated together in five metal burial vaults, their bones and fluids commingled in a horrid stew.

Next door a greasy liquid layered the concrete floor of the main crematory building, and a hole had been hand-cut into the baseboard to allow for drainage. (A normal crematory requires no special drainage, as the extreme temperatures of incineration leave only a solid residue as described earlier.) Six bodies in various stages of decomposition waited near the retort, or kiln, which itself held a single corpse in a cardboard cremation box. Important paperwork littered the premises.

The smaller shed contained two more mummified bodies discovered beneath more trash, and outside stood a hearse carrying another corpse. This solitary individual had lain in the vehicle since 1998, dressed in his funeral clothes inside a casket. For some reason, after making one last pickup, Brent Marsh had abandoned both the man and his carriage.

The wider circle of woods featured other rusted automobiles and a house trailer, along with randomly dispersed body bags and coffins, exposed bodies and limbs, isolated bones. Dirt paths wound through the grounds, and along one such path a single body lay embedded, like a speed bump for the backhoe, packed tight. And beneath more trash moldered eight mass graves, dug to an average depth of five feet.

In one pit, where twenty-three bodies were eventually recovered, the identification process proved difficult. As Dr. Kris Sperry, the chief medical examiner for the state of Georgia, explained, "The bodies that went into that particular pit may well have been put in one of the vaults for a period of time, where they decomposed down to a horrendous mess, and then the vault was upended and poured into the pit."

Twenty-three individuals were also recovered from the immediate area surrounding an old pool table. The felt board lay upside down, and rotting tarpaulins and rope suggested an attempt to create a nest, or basket, from the table's legs. Most of these bodies were unclothed, and the bones and flesh were severely commingled, with animal scavenging separating limbs and helping to cause the heavier bones to drift to the bottom. Here the seasonal deposit of pine needles and oak leaves helped to delineate individuals, providing an identifying layer, a stratum, for the dumped bodies.

A few yards from the pool table site, debris—including food, logs, clothing, large appliances, fencing, and tires— combined with bones in an intricate tangle. Shallow trenches stretched below that trash, housing more corpses.

Nearly all these pits lay fairly close to the crematory buildings. One, however, was found fewer than ninety feet from Brent Marsh's residence, in the dense brush next to the lake.

Given these details, a broad divergence of opinion emerged concerning the cause of Brent Marsh's actions during his alchemical period. Several former and current FBI profilers contended that he was simply "disorganized" and "lazy," and that he internally rationalized his actions by focusing on the fact that the bodies only "belonged to dead people."

Some analyses were less psychological, more pragmatic. "The whole situation reminds me of an office worker who gets behind on his paperwork so he chucks it in a drawer," commented State Representative Doug Teper upon officially touring the Tri-State property. "After a while, he's spending more time finding new places to hide his papers than on doing any actual work."

In contrast, as I learned from the *Atlanta Journal-Constitution*—my source of much information regarding the incident—a psychology professor specializing in anxiety disorders at the University of Georgia, Nader Amir, suggested that Brent Marsh may have suffered from the obsessive-compulsive disorder known as "hoarding." As Professor Amir stated, "People with this problem keep things they don't need . . . It's not that they're really lazy, they just can't make a decision [about what to discard]. It gets harder and harder and the hoarding continues." Indeed, the vast disorganization at the site—combined with Marsh's actual cremation of two-thirds of the bodies during the period—made the analysis sound compelling to me. And yet a couple of things ran counter to this argument. Beyond the evident chaos, Brent Marsh acted with premeditation in his meticulous development and deployment of fake cremains, and, quite clearly and inexcusably, he exhibited a real cold-bloodedness in his disregard of hundreds of bodies. And yet again, in support of the hoarding hypothesis, why bother cremating only a percentage of available bodies when the math made no rational sense in the first place?

I kept going back to the emptiness—to the gaze—to the eyes that appeared so vacant. Whatever the primary impetus for his actions (and unlike the early alchemists), Brent Marsh apparently did not include the attainment of higher consciousness in his calculus. Instead, as the numbers piled up, he may have been attempting to impose a kind of order in his life, however strange and unsettling. I mean, the guy wasn't a psycho-killer—he hadn't murdered anyone—but for a long time he'd looked past the sanctity of flesh toward something else. Some deeper focus. The key lay at the end of that stare.

6

~~

MY MOTHER RANG the West Coast and said I needed to get back fast—he might not last the weekend.

From thirty thousand miles up I watched the land turn from brown to green, worrying obsessively that he might not recognize me.

Outside the door was one world: a place I knew—the hospital where I'd come with my cracked wrist after falling drunk from a moving car in tenth grade and where I'd received a few stitches for a knife wound to a finger sustained by my own hand, the other hand, while doing a stupid *Huckleberry Finn* diorama in eleventh grade.

Inside there was another world: the place where I'd see my father for the last time. When I'd left a few weeks before, he still looked pretty good—a too-thin man on the verge, a goner—but he was still Ron Hendricks; he was still my father. Now his body was not his body—not my father—but a shriveled-up thing on white sheets, his bones curled like a child's. In that quicker light only his face looked familiar, stretched and smeared across a gray skull with blotches.

Without opening his eyes, he somehow found my hand and held on to it.

"Brent," he whispered in a far-off voice.

"I'm here," I said.

I waited as he cleared layers of sediment from his throat.

"You've been a good boy." Then he let go of my hand and curled up tighter, falling back into his death dream.

After my mother and sister went home to rest, I looked out from the fourth floor at the highway's edge—the same highway, I-400, where I'd sat in the backseat of a drag-racing Dodge Charger as it flew across the empty pavement at 120 mph—the lanes now stacked with rush-hour traffic creeping north. As it grew dark, I watched the feathery seeds of cottonwoods rise over and over against the high glass.

He was only fifty-nine: a skeleton and not a man. And though I knew it was self-centered, I couldn't help but wonder if I'd look like him when I died—when I died too young.

Now his breathing seemed a little worse but it didn't matter. A levee of morphine held back the pain. All life support had been taken off so it was up to him—up to his heart and maybe his brain. Maybe Jesus. My father, it seemed, had gotten a touch of religion over these last few years: not much, not the churchgoing kind, but he'd started reading Scripture again and talking about it. Every now and then I'd see his arm twitch, his legs move a little. He made no sounds except for the breathing.

If I said goodbye, I don't remember. We thought we still had a couple days to go. So when some friends took over the night shift, I got on that highway and tried to forget—crawling past my old exit, Northridge Road, past the lights of my school, Crestwood High School, past the dead ends lying out there in the clustered bands of suburban and now exurban development, until the traffic finally broke and I revved along back roads to my parents' new house in the mountains.

A gated community, Big Canoe was actually a seven-mountain resort whose name strove to recall the more natural and rustic days of Cherokee habitation, but not so natural as to exclude golf, tennis (indoor and outdoor), swimming (pool and lake), a general store, a chapel, and a cemetery. I tried to distract myself from my father by thinking of the other things living and dying out there—of the terrible drought that had squeezed Georgia for several years now, that had subsided with some rain in late spring, but in October 1990 reappeared with a vengeance. To save themselves, many of the shadowy oaks I passed had probably changed color early: green to rust-red, green to orange.

At the five-bedroom cabin, a house built on stilts, we communicated like people do in these situations—mostly gestures and eyes—and after a while I poured another glass of my father's top-shelf Evan Williams whiskey and stepped out onto the back porch.

It was glorious out there: In daylight you could see all the way to North Carolina and Tennessee; you could see the water plummet over Amicalola Falls twenty miles away. Turkey vultures zoomed by at eye level. Bears rustled through mountain laurel below. And now at night it was an impossible firmament of stars in which the Milky Way, in its particular brightness, looked very much like the real road to heaven.

When we got the call, however, I left that scene and marched straight through the front door and started screaming. A howl and then a moan and then a wail. Not a grief-stricken letting-go—not a release born from love—but a voice that tore out of me like an animal. Like a body. Like a thing that was not me, vanishing where it rose into the dry trees.

There was another story about my father and a drought—and then the opposite of a drought—that until the bizarre tales surrounding his death had long been my main story about him. It began with his birth in 1931, at the opening of the Great Depression, and described his family's hardscrabble life on a hardscrabble farm in Oklahoma. The farm lay north of Tulsa, and every day dust clouds filled the sky like Old Testament locusts, bringing plague and hunger and bankruptcy. Eventually my grandparents gave up the farm, and my grandfather, a Church of God choir member with a booming voice, took a series of oil field jobs in Oklahoma: Nowata, Cleveland, and ultimately Sapulpa. And after the war, the Army Corps of Engineers, in its great midcentury zeal for altering the American terrain, flooded the old farm and the surrounding region. The corps built an earthen dam on the Verdigris River that buried the land underwater, erasing that place from the map forever.

My bones dropped when I heard this story as a kid. Secretly, I played out its apocalyptic details.

From my treeless suburban backyard in Bartlesville, Oklahoma (where my father worked as branch manager of IBM), I imagined dust clouds building on the horizon and pictured my grandmother sweeping the thick dust from a dirt floor, dust that blew through every crevice and hole in the tiny farmhouse. Then, when the clouds passed over—a decadal shift that occurred instantaneously in my child's brain—the dust turned suddenly to water and I walked under it; the sky shifted to lake surface and I trudged beneath it, churning my arms. After slogging up and down my underwater yard for a while, I'd race toward the back door, my lungs bursting. Surely my mother thought me a little peculiar: a small boy who kept crashing into the air-conditioned den, gulping for air.

When I was young, I always wanted my father to return to that place and that water. I remember asking him, without success, to take us to Oologah Lake sometime so

I could see it. (Strangely, the lake was named after the Cherokee word for "dark cloud"—and just as a black cloud hung over my fabled Cherokee relatives who were kicked out of Georgia and forced upon the Trail of Tears to Oklahoma, so a dark cloud gathered over my father's entrance to and exit from this world.) And then once we'd moved farther away—once I'd become more conscious of my own displacement as a teenager haunting those Atlanta dead ends—the watery scene bloomed into something of an obsession, like being buried alive.

So I'd daydream about my father going back, down to the lake bottom where he was born.

I'd imagine him trudging past a country gas station and general store, stumbling out toward a tin mailbox with the route number worn clean, where bloated cows hovered in his own father's fields. And I'd see him climb onto the front steps of the porch, open the screen door, sit down to wait in the sunken rooms.

The chapel was packed. A Presbyterian missionary, Wayne Smith, a friend of my parents and a member of Jimmy Carter's religious circle, began his eulogy with a story about my father, Jesus, and golf.

Apparently, after his death, my father appeared to Reverend Smith on one of the shorter three-par holes at Big Canoe. My father returned to say that Jesus was real— His love was real—and then I think someone (either my father or the reverend) made a hole in one. As that miraculous tale unfolded, however, my mind drifted back to the drought—to the oaks that had in fact changed color early, shading orange and red beyond the chapel door. I jerked myself to attention. I tried to focus.

But it didn't help that the casket remained shut, draped in roses and lilies that hung nearly to the floor. I felt agitated and jumpy. I didn't like that veil over his body.

And I didn't want to hear about golf or my father's good deeds. I didn't want to think about the drought or the pretty colors of fall.

I wanted more. There had to be more. I wanted to be with him now in this place. I wanted to experience the dead and the living together—to become more alive in that opening unto death—even to become death for a moment. It was the most a body could do, I decided, watching Jesus floating high on the chapel wall, nailed to a couple of boards. It would be my inheritance.

But as they lowered him into the ground, I learned something about myself. I learned I was a coward. I tried to imagine my father's body but I couldn't do it. I couldn't get closer to his shriveled-up chest and slender bones. I couldn't open the door of that coffin, feel the sway of muscle and tendon, the great transacting of flesh into dirt.

And then to make amends for that error, I made another. I panicked. I tried to summon my love for the man again—to feel some love—and when that didn't arrive I panicked more and turned off. Nothing washed over or passed through me. Not Jesus love or Father love or some Universal-type love. I didn't feel anything at all.

The flag was folded up. The pile of earth was ready. And I thought how beautiful the resort cemetery looked—a wild clearing in the woods traversed by meditation benches and flat granite markers. No wildflowers this time of year, just trees and bushes that looked exhausted.

IN MEMORY OF RONALD CASTO HENDRICKS

1931–1990

They put the stone down when we were gone.

7

〜

DE SOTO WOULD NEVER FIND HIS GOLD. He would travel throughout the South and he would not find what he was looking for. But early on he didn't know this, of course. He was voracious and he was invincible. And when he heard about a treasure lode of freshwater pearls, he acted swiftly. At a mortuary house near the Wateree River, his soldiers pried open stacked wooden boxes and tore the pearls from the bodies of the dead—two hundred pounds' worth, much of it darkened and stained by years of lying against rotting flesh. Men of providence, they took the pearls when they had the chance.

8

~~~

MOTORBOATS ZOOMED over the smooth water of Lake Tuscaloosa, bearing skiers who vectored random arrows across the black surface. Amid this playful scene, it was difficult to remember that a relentless drought gripped western Alabama, among the worst of the past century. It was difficult to remember because this was a fake lake, a large reservoir formed by a dam, which due to its very immensity had shown only a small drop under the severest of drought conditions. This was all good, of course, for boaters and Tuscaloosans who could go about their business as if the climate remained unstressed, whizzing around in their speedboats and inundating their big lawns daily.

Such dams were not so good, however, for the wildlife here and elsewhere across the greater Mobile Bay Basin; as a matter of fact, we had apocalypse, mostly of the smooth fake-lake variety.

The primary victims were freshwater snails and mussels, drowned by the deepwater dams of the regional power companies and/or the Army Corps of Engineers. These species needed free-flowing water to reproduce and thrive, especially shoals where shallow water raced over rocks. Scores of different kinds of bodies had vanished— more than fifty separate species along the Coosa River alone, a tributary of the basin, making the event a truly momentous one in the history of the living earth. In short, biologists considered the Coosa die-off among the worst North American mass extinctions since the demise of the dinosaurs over sixty-five million years ago.

Some of those drowned mussels would be carrying freshwater pearls, the same pretty orbs prized by both Natives and invaders. In a concordance of destruction, it was the Coosa that de Soto followed as he marched into Alabama.

And with all the straightening and dredging and damming of the Black Warrior, the South sacrificed one of its most beautiful rivers. Once upon a time above Tuscaloosa, the Black Warrior consisted of a series of twelve shoals or rapids wandering southward, some as wide as a thousand feet. Waterfalls and streaming gorges cascaded down high bluffs on either bank. And in one location, the world's largest stand of shoal lilies—a three-foot-tall tapestry of flowers springing from a sandstone riverbed—once bloomed its white, complicated blooms in the month of May.

Now the graveyard of that expanse of white blossoms lay at the bottom of another fake lake: a thin blue spot on my map. Now only the ghosts of those flowers moved delicately underwater, swaying their perfect white heads.

It was May and the ghost lilies would be in high bloom.

For a moment I considered a short detour to gaze at the smooth water—pay my respects to a stand of white petals once the broadest and loveliest on earth. But not now, I decided. I needed to stay on my path. I needed to find another haunted place in the deeper hills.

Directly behind the main building at the Tri-State Crematory stood another fake lake—small enough, I suppose, to be called a pond. Such private bodies of water were common in the South. Homeowners liked to stock the dredged pits with fish and, if there weren't too many snakes around, take a dip in their own personal swimming holes.

On Center Point Road in Noble, Georgia, the lake functioned as the focal point of the Marshes' sixteen-acre spread. At the east end of the lake, Ray Marsh had built the Tri-State Crematory in 1981. The main building rested close to the water down a long driveway, and the two outbuildings stood nearby. Ray and his wife, Clara, lived in a small house adjacent to the crematory property. His daughter LeShea also lived there. And eventually Brent Marsh settled one door down in a handsome stone house that backed up to the lake.

For good reason, the Georgia Bureau of Investigation had strong suspicions about the Marshes' lake. When they first searched the grounds, authorities found a human torso and skull floating near a hidden bank, as well as many intact skeletons strewn in the surrounding brush. It was no stretch, then, to fear that Brent Marsh had stuffed bodies inside metal burial vaults, just as he'd done on land, and then dumped the loaded vaults into the water.

In the early days of Tri-State, I believed they'd find my father's body under that lake. It made sense—the final place of unrest for a restless man. He'd been born into a place and the big machines had taken that place away. A biblical-style deluge had come, though unlike after that Great Flood there'd been no promise not to flood the world again.

And I think his personal flood set him loose, forever cutting his ties with the land. He could never go back to the old farm and fill his present with pictures of the past—never find a familiar slope of ground, a stand of known wildflowers, a beautiful curve of a blackjack tree. He never talked of that first home or any other place from his childhood. He never told me about a house or a yard or a garden or a field. No animals and no friends. He never told me any stories from his childhood, none at all—it was my mother who told the story about the flood—as if every image from that time had been erased by those apocalyptic waters.

In fact, I wanted them to find my father dreaming in the depths of Brent Marsh's lake. Of course to everyone else, especially my mother, it seemed like an awful possibility—bodies rotting together in a packed vault lodged in snake-filled black water. But for me it would frame his beginning as well as his end, and create some order where there was none.

———

A helicopter news camera distinctly showed the pines that ringed the black surface and the reflection of ragged branches against the sky. Later, only a glimmer of the lake's jagged shape emerged by Internet satellite. And finally the lake did not appear at all in the photograph of the newly bulldozed field I carried on my pilgrimage day. Instead the lake floated beyond that picture, just beyond the field where most of the decaying corpses once lay in dense woods next to the crematory driveway.

And while the actual image receded, the myth of the fake lake continued to accelerate, a growing strand in a tangle of Tri-State images. Over time I even developed my own esotericism on the subject, conjecturing that a fake lake's membrane, always of the smooth variety, offered two distinct pathways: a mirror to the sky or a window to some unknown depth. Reflection or passage. Up or down. Your primary orientation, I theorized, had a lot to do with who you were.

And the utter emptiness of Brent Marsh's face allowed for such projection. Did he kneel by the shoreline, for example, and gaze into the pond's flat glass? Did he trace the pines and oaks that framed a halo against the sky? Or, after a long day of digging and dumping and alchemical blending of concrete dust and bone, did he just stare at his own face blankly—his blank face gazing back—his picture always sliding away beneath deeper water?

9

〰

THE SHIT FAIRY'S EARLIEST RECORDED VISIT to our family came in 1983. Though no one in the family knows exactly when, or how, that mystical being received its name in the greater world, we now understand that year to be the opening address to our family, the initial appearance of the uninvited guest.

I was finishing my first year of law school when I got the call. My mother had metastasized breast cancer and she'd probably die. Chemotherapy. Radiation. Surgery. Round after round. And then, without notice, the Shit Fairy vanished, leaving my mother alive (and still alive today) to identify her malefactor.

To me, the Shit Fairy was simply a name given to misfortune. It was a blackly funny metaphor about a human inevitability: Bad things would happen to you that were out of your control. My mother would get cancer by virtue of the Shit Fairy's appearance, and then her body, bolstered by a good immune system or the former's exit, would do its best to fight off the disease. Sometimes you'd lose and sometimes you wouldn't. And then sometimes the Shit Fairy would throw you a bizarrely inexplicable event—maybe an event lying somewhere between life and death, or more accurately death and then another death— like abandoning your father's body at the Tri-State Crematory for five years. And though the entity itself provided no real supernatural solace, you could say the name out loud and the saying provided some comfort. Somehow, somewhere, consolation lay in the words.

By all accounts my mother seemed to have acquired the term from friends. But beyond that, where did the title come from? Did the Shit Fairy have any historical or legendary parallels? It was, after all, a "fairy," and a long past existed concerning such beings.

Searching for predecessors, I found that many southeastern tribes told variant stories of the Little People, and as I had at least one legendary ancestor among the Cherokees, I was especially interested to find their connection to that tribe. For the Cherokees, the Little People were largely good-natured folk who lived in undeveloped places such as rocky cliffs and caves. They assisted humans in many ways—gathering corn in the dead of night, or guiding lost children through the mountain forest. Only if mentioned by name or disturbed in their homes did the Cherokee Little People cause problems, and then events we might today attribute to bad luck—broken bones, illness, death—would be charged to them. I wondered if my north Atlanta suburb—born of digging and scraping and moving the earth—had disturbed an ancient dwelling place of the Little People, if the Shit Fairy had marked us for a visit way back then.

I thought of the Shit Fairy as I rolled into the Alabama countryside, climbing higher into the Piedmont plateau, because of the heavy flowering of churches along the road. Whereas my family of lapsed Presbyterians had the Shit Fairy to explain events—a theology based solely on the personification of bad luck—most Southerners had Jesus to ascribe causation to. And out here the houses of Jesus, the churches, grew more dominant as the ground became more hilly and the broken-down mobile homes proliferated in the exposed dirt—exposed either from erosion, backhoe, or simple neglect and then dotted with black-eyed Susans. Which is not to say there were more churches in the country than in the city or the suburbs—Tuscaloosa County as a whole boasted over three hundred houses of Christian worship—just that they stood out against the sad and scarred land, the lush and yet weirdly unbeautiful land.

Nailed to a pine tree on the right side of the road, a white sheet of paper asked that I *Please worship God and Jesus.* It was one of maybe a dozen I'd seen since the suburbs—handwritten messages on regular copy paper fastened to trees and fence posts. Edicts in black marker sent directly from the Holy Ghost, they said things like *Please do God's work as he wants you to* and *Please do what God tells you to do* and *Thank God for the gift of Jesus* and *Please do God's will today.* Someone certainly had gotten the Spirit and needed to tell the driving public all about it. And as strangely unbeautiful as the land along the highway appeared, gouged and neglected, these pieces of paper actually were beautiful. Almost transparent in the morning sun, black letters floating against wood, they seemed like little flags of the apocalypse, gently prodding us to be good.

New stands of short pines rose from timber company clear-cuts. A black rectangle of an old trampoline leaned against a worn-out brick house with too many inhabitants and too many cars. A place called Sunshine Valley offered lots and mobile homes for rent, while the Piney Woods Church, a nineteenth-century brown brick church with a well-tended cemetery on the other side of the two-lane, offered some version of salvation.

I say "version" because there are so many churches with varying practices in the county. It's nearly impossible to appreciate the cultural dominance of Christianity in the Protestant South—the felt presence—unless you've spent some time here. Only years of exposure might enable one to navigate the theological distinctions among, say, the Church of Christ, Church of God, Church of God-in-Christ, and Church of God-of-Prophecy. The general demographics present an easier account.

I know, for example, that over fifty percent of Alabama's citizens characterize themselves as fundamentalist—believing in the literal truth of the Bible, the word-for-word truth—a figure three times greater than that found in a progressive state like Massachusetts. Fundamentalists, however, are not to be confused with evangelicals. The former merely occupy the right wing of the evangelical movement, a movement that also includes liberal Democrats and moderates like Jimmy Carter. And yet the movement is not so heterogeneous as some like to maintain. Across the nation as a whole, five times more evangelicals describe themselves as conservatives than as liberals.

Beliefs, of course, have practical effects—for better or for worse—and one particularly conservative church has held sway in this part of the country since before the Civil War.

In fact, a good deal of the existing cultural disturbance in the Deep South can be tied to the historical efforts of the Southern Baptists. This statement is hardly controversial. The political influence of the group cannot be minimized, particularly regarding the very place I now drove through. Sometimes called the "State Church of Alabama," the Southern Baptists, just over a decade ago, claimed membership of one in four Alabamians and two in three of the state's churchgoing citizens. (More recently, the huge nondenominational churches, mostly fundamentalist in their own right, had appropriated a portion of the Baptists' traditional constituency.) Unfortunately, at every juncture the Southern Baptist Convention (SBC)—the umbrella organization of affiliated churches—employed its broad influence to usurp basic civil liberties. The scars left by its actions are as evident as, and entwined with, those left on the land by poverty, unbridled development, dams, extinctions, and the nearby strip-mining for Alabama's high-grade coal.

And yet unlike the Shit Fairy's, the denomination's origin and history are well documented. In 1845, Southern Baptists broke away from the national organization because the rest of the country's Baptists, particularly those in New England, would not sanction slaveholding missionaries. Thus the Southern Baptists emerged as a staunchly proslavery group and based their defense of that practice on a "literal" interpretation of the Bible. Specifically, the SBC pointed to Noah's condemning of Canaan, the son of Ham and presumed progenitor of the black race, as the "servant" of "his brethren." (Canaan, it appears, deserved such a fate—along with the millions of Africans born to slavery and degradation in the future—because Ham had seen the nakedness of his drunk father, Noah, and had not seemed particularly embarrassed by it.)

Armed with the "firmly established" scriptural belief that God intended slavery, and that African Americans were inferior, the SBC fought hard against racial equality at every step in Southern history. First, their spiritual backing of slavery provided a religious underpinning for the Civil War. Later, having lost that argument, the Southern

Baptists maintained that the Bible condoned—indeed, ordained—segregation. In this way, emboldened by religious zealotry, the SBC would struggle against federal antilynching laws, desegregation, and all manner of civil rights well into the second half of the twentieth century. Over time, the actions of the Southern Baptists put them directly at odds with historically separate black Baptist congregations, such as Martin Luther King's Ebenezer Baptist Church in Atlanta.

When my parents moved us to our Atlanta suburb, they decided to repent of their fallen Presbyterianism and attend a nearby church on Sunday. They had never been big believers—in fact I don't recall a single act of Christian instruction in the home—but I think they felt the need to ease the dislocation of our constant movement, to provide some stable ground for themselves and their children.

I remember the day well. Decked out in our new Sunday clothes, my sister and I groaned as we buckled in to our red Toyota wagon and headed off to the local Presbyterian church. Located in a renovated brick building, this house of worship was successfully making its way from an old country church to a more affluent suburban one. A brand-new fancy mall, Perimeter Mall (where my sister and I had bought our new clothes), had recently sprung up nearby. My parents no doubt expected a bland sermon from the New South, with little or no dogmatic fire. And yet, as we sat together in the crowded pews, the minister declaimed the same segregationist doctrine of African American inferiority that had been the mainstay of the Southern Baptists. In fact, at a moment of emphatic crescendo, this emissary of Jesus actually used the n-word.

My parents flinched. My soon-to-be-hippie sister turned red with anger. And we marched straight out of that church and never went back. On that day, the Shit Fairy smiled with Shit Fairy glee. And the turbulent ground my parents had hoped to steady, tamed by Jesus, shook with a vengeance.

Traveling northward along Highway 69, I passed the Windham Springs Baptist Church, one of scores of Baptist churches I knew I'd encounter on my short trip. Suddenly, on the western side of the road, toward Mississippi, a wave of flags appeared against the trees. Eight Confederate Battle Flags strapped to eight different poles. They flew brilliantly above an encampment of mobile homes and beat-up trucks and cars where a few regular-looking guys (one in fatigues and one with a University of Alabama ball cap) leaned over the popped hood of a full-size pickup.

I wanted to slow down, to take it all in, to study the faces of these modern-day Confederates. I wanted to stop and ask them exactly what they believed they were doing, whom they were fighting for and fighting against. I wanted to be sure. Nearly 150 years after the war, why were these guys still playing army? And yet I knew that inside their decrepit homes, these men had most likely amassed a very real Confederate arsenal. Probably shotguns and semiautomatic handguns, a good old-fashioned assault rifle or two. I wasn't black or Mexican, but with my citified looks as well as my poorly folded American flag in the front seat of my Swedish car, I didn't suppose I'd be too welcome. And anyway, didn't I know what they were fighting for and what that flag was all about? Hadn't the modern racists entirely co-opted the meaning of the flag during the civil rights era? Hadn't the old lines of power been sanctioned and affirmed not so long ago?

I sped on. That band of Confederate irregulars never glanced up. And soon their image faded into a row of oak-leaf hydrangea, the ragged state wildflower of Alabama that grew in all types of ground (disturbed and nondisturbed areas). In the month of May, these sprawling bushes bloomed spiky white flowers that later turned a deep rose. This particular state flower, my field guide explained, was a shade plant that couldn't handle much direct sun.

10

I PASSED A PAIR of blue-lettered Ten Commandments tablets displayed prominently like FOR SALE signs in an ugly yard. *Honor thy father*, I said to myself, picturing the Shit Fairy straddling two heavy chloroplast tablets.

Born of dirt-poor parents during the heart of the Great Depression, my father was the youngest of five brothers—thirteen years younger than his nearest brother, making him a "mistake" by his own admission. (As a child, I spent some time wondering exactly what this mistake was.) When his father finally got an oil field job, a decent union job, his family moved around northeast Oklahoma following the rigs. Yet the only other detail I recall was the one about the lake—how the Army Corps of Engineers flooded the farm he'd lived on for the first years of his life.

Once my mother came along, so came the stories and a clearer picture of his life. When my father moved to town, as my mother tells it, she quickly claimed him as her own, and the two were sweethearts by age sixteen. I have some old photographs of them from that time, one printed in the local newspaper in 1948.

In this particular photograph, my father, a star end on the high school football team, lies sprawled on the sidelines after a touchdown. A kid trainer in a letter jacket leans over him, holding a rag against his broken nose, as my father's only visible eye rolls high into his knocked-out brain. And with gloved hands on her thick skirt, my mother kneels down to him, her pretty face so rapt as to be expressionless. On this cold football night, however, my father rises from the ground at the call of the coach—rises right out of this photograph because he's the kicker and has to kick off. He rises right out of the sports pages and wanders onto the wrong side of the field. When his teammates finally catch up to him, he's led away, disoriented and dazed, relegated to the sidelines for the rest of the game.

Though his own father had completed only the eighth grade, and his older brothers only high school, he worked hard to put himself through Oklahoma State University. He even became the Lucky Strike distributor on campus, a showy sales job with the bonus of free cigarettes. And in a practice common during the period, my parents married after my mother's sophomore year, and she dropped out to support his career. In the end my father proved worthy of the sacrifice: He was ROTC, president of his fraternity, and eventually president of the student body. He also got good grades, and the door swung open.

Before beginning a job at IBM, however, my father had to complete his stint in the service. In 1954 he was sent to Forbes Air Force Base in Topeka. Forbes was a new arm of the Strategic Air Command, the military structure designated to deliver a first-strike nuclear knockout of the Soviet Union. Assigned to the 55th Strategic Reconnaissance Wing, my father and the other airmen wore a uniform patch boasting WE SEE ALL. And, commensurate with their motto, they did their best to see all. A few times a week my father flew his B-47 Stratojet—a converted high-performance bomber known for its precarious landings—all the way to the edge of the Soviet Empire and back. In the reconnaissance planes, the bomb bay, designed to hold a single nuclear explosive, was remade to house an intelligence officer who operated the extensive system of cameras in the plane's nose. On flying days, my pilot father shepherded his plane over the Arctic to the Baltic coast, where the radar and telescopic cameras diligently tracked the nuclear activity of the Communist enemy.

My father was scared to death on those flights. He hated them. Though not terrified of flying, he was terrified of piloting those big jets. And yet in an assertion backed up by my mother to this day, my father proudly claimed he occasionally carried nuclear bombs on board.

"The Big One," he told me once. "I carried the Big One."

And yet from my research, I really don't think his nuclear recollection was true—there seemed to have been no crossover between the bomber and reconnaissance wings even on the same base. Was it possible he didn't know, some sort of military double trick?

Or maybe the first burst of honesty about his fear allowed him the less-honest boast about bombs, as if he were keeping a rough moral ledger in his head somewhere. And regardless, it's not as if a white lie—even one with potentially blinding light—violated any particular commandment. More important to me, the image connected the larger picture of my father to my incipient notion of the ultimate doomsday machinery, to the end that might one day arrive from the sky.

After the Air Force, and the birth of that little white lie concerning nuclear bombs, objectively my father's experience was all about IBM. He worked there for thirty years, moving his family to five corporate destinations and five bigger houses by the time I entered the seventh grade.

And as with the subject of his childhood, he didn't talk about the details of his job. He left for work at seven in the morning and returned twelve hours later. Though he wanted to do so, he never grew a mustache because it was against corporate policy. He worked hard and made pretty good money. And when he turned forty, he suddenly realized he would not be president of IBM because he didn't have an MBA; he realized (most likely the last to know) that he would not ascend the corporate ladder beyond upper-level management in his huge division. After that he hated his job, just like he hated flying those dangerous planes, but he kept doing it. That was that, a life behind a veil.

And yet in his practice of photography, according to my own narrative of his life, he did reveal more about the forces that moved him. The hobby started early on, when he began his corporate job with its bigger paycheck. Very quickly my father became a fanatic, purchasing multiple cameras and multiple lenses, multiple tripods and multiple flashes. Multiple everything in a rush of high-powered consumerism. On a Saturday, it was not uncommon for him to be tromping around the house with three camera bags strapped to his back, hunting for an angle of me shooting baskets or my sister practicing her various cheers. There was so much jumbling and focusing and clicking we grew accustomed to the stagelike atmosphere: We thought everyone lived the life of pictures.

As a smaller child, I especially liked the attention. Being photographed was just another way to spend some time with my father. Despite his busy job and furious weekend projects (mowing and planting, tuning his sports car, hammering—I remember a lot of hammering), he always seemed to have enough hours for me. In spring and summer we tossed baseballs back and forth across the yard, in summer we threw footballs, and in winter we arced basketballs into the colder air. We kept the ritual of the seasons as well as any earthly gods might do. And honestly,

I never felt neglected by a lack of interest. With his enormous energy, his restlessness and can-do attitude, he always managed to fit me in. And he liked it, too, he liked me and he liked showing me how to do things. And of course he was at all my kid games, clicking away.

But as I got older, those same father-son activities evolved into pressurized lessons regarding proper form and, especially, the correct "mental mind-set" of a winner. His go-getter insistence shifted playtime into a test and expectation of high performance. And when it turned out I excelled at all that athletic stuff, my father became even more serious about my "training." On the weekends or in the half dark after dinner, I endured detailed lessons regarding my batting stance, the angle of my throwing arm, my inadequate and trembling will.

I recall the particular day our sessions turned from play to work, or at least the day I realized things had changed. On a Saturday, in springtime, my father put his glittering cameras and lenses on the couch—he would return to these soon enough—and asked me to grab my bat and our bag of scuffed baseballs. I noticed my sister doing something in the shade behind the house as my father and I lined up in our usual positions. An old oak tree acted as our backstop, the only big tree left standing in our corner of the newly flattened Missouri subdivision. I was nine years old.

The night before, it seems, I had made a great mistake. For some reason I'd been placed on a team with older kids and under the lights I had embarrassed my father. When I came up to bat for the first time in the last inning, the bases loaded and the game tied, the Jolly Rogers' pitcher suddenly loomed too tall against the night's glare and the mound looked too close. The ball made an electric whizzing, and a terrible thud broke behind me when it crossed the plate.

And I—faced with the wild heat of that big kid, his arm born of speed and lightning—I started to shake. My father stopped shooting and I began to cry. The clattering of our game died away. And eventually my manager tried to console me, the umpire tried to console me, and that Jolly Rogers giant, discomposed by all the commotion, walked me in for the winning run. But when I slunk back toward the dugout, I could see my father smoldering behind the screen.

In the sharp light of the next spring day, however, my father appeared to have forgotten the event. As usual—though it sounds so bizarre today—he asked me about the difference between a hurt and an injury, to which I replied, "An injury leaves a scar." It was what I was told to say. It was all part of the litany, part of the ritual. But when I stepped into my small batter's box made out of sticks, he added, "Well, Brent, it's time you learned to hold your ground."

I don't know how long I stood there. Or how many pitches struck me in the back, as I spun, or on my legs. But I stood there awhile. And my father, his voice now disconnected from his body, yelled not to step out of the batter's box or he'd throw even harder. He said not to cry because these were only "hurts" that would go away.

But I did begin to cry, and the balls kept pounding me in my little box. I did cry as the balls flew faster in the morning sun.

Ultimately, it was my eleven-year-old sister who sprang to the rescue. She began screaming at my father to leave me alone, her voice mixing with his in the air above our heads, and my mother ran out to stop the game. Later, perhaps prodded by my mother, my father did offer a degree of conciliation—he bought me a new glove and took my picture.

Today, of course, parents are more informed about the dangers of overinvolvement and overidentification with their kids, but not so long ago it was different. My father didn't especially know it might be a mistake to turn a sports-minded child into an object of performance. And I don't mean to suggest he was the worst example of that, either—he had too much social sense to embarrass either of us by some public haranguing. Instead, after the ball-throwing episode, on the postgame car rides home it was always the deep analysis and criticism of my play first and then some compliment about the better things. The successful things. The bad always took precedence over the good, as if hitting a baseball were some type of a career for a little kid. And later in Atlanta, when I turned to junior tennis and became one of the best players in the South, the heavy-handed guidance blossomed into an identifiable obsession on my father's part. He now had two obsessions: his photography and me. I felt the pressure of his constant critique and voracious judgment.

Beginning with that makeshift baseball field in the backyard, a hard ground grew between me and my father, a distance that lengthened to unhappy proportions. Though damaging in its own right, this distance did have the benefit of forestalling the father-son altercations so common during the teenage years. No fists or bruises, as several of my close friends reported. No yelling contests. No pointed dinnertime glares. Instead, my revolt—and my father's response—understandably reflected the political reality of our more nuanced, cold war strategic theater.

Rather than bombs, then, the struggle for boundaries and spheres of influence took on a psychodramatic character. In short, following the dictates of mutually assured destruction (MAD, a term every newspaper-reading thirteen-year-old understood), we needed each other to sustain existence.

On his side of the war, each weekend my father poured a bath of chemicals in his darkroom and lifted my face to air—an image strikingly resembling his own—and in doing so re-created himself in the thin red atmosphere of our planet. No longer was he simply a paper-pushing manager at IBM, stuck in a lifeless Georgia suburb defined solely by material consumption, but an agent of intimacy always creating a new self, a form that conveniently looked a lot like him. And dependent as he was on me for his very identity, this overidentification required that no traditional father-son bombings take place. With our selves so commingled and confused, any open confrontation remained too risky.

My strategy—following the same MAD principle—was seemingly to go along with it all. At school I was the model student (best grades, best attitude). After school I was the burgeoning tennis champion, doing hours of drills and practice matches at the local tennis academy. In the early evening I'd report back to my liaison, providing detailed information about my subject's comings and goings. And though a double agent who reported extensively on his own activities, I was something else. I was also an agent who worked for the *other* other side: the teenager's side.

In the dark, I'd slip away to smoke pot in the cul-de-sac or make out with a girlfriend. On weekends, I'd often drink too many tall boys, and as I vomited my secrets out the window, a friend would drive me home through the twisted roads of kudzu and pines. I began listening to Lou Reed and the Velvet Underground. I began listening to the Grateful Dead.

And ironically, the years-long war of surveillance and shifting identities took its toll on my father's most prized investment: my tennis career. I could never develop my own player's identity to suit my talents. On consecutive days I'd try to *be*, not just copy, Ilie Nastase (my favorite with his artful nonchalance), Björn Borg (the stoic warrior with implacable footwork), and Guillermo Vilas (the long-haired poet with the heavy one-handed topspin backhand). Though I had some success, eventually ranked #1 in Georgia and #2 in the South, my coaches grew increasingly frustrated. I just couldn't sustain a consistent self-image as a performer. With so many conflicting pictures floating around inside my head, I developed a chronic and incurable version of tennis player's multiple personality disorder.

The worst part of my privileged story—the part that added fuel to my proliferation of selves—was that my father appeared to be the best father. He was the father my friends all wanted to have! From the outside, he seemed neither despot nor disciplinarian—he never grounded me for missing curfew, for example; he never bullied me about school. He didn't create arbitrary rules to test my allegiance. No, our entanglement was much more sophisticated. Who needed silly rules when you'd already put into place a panopticon-like surveillance system in which your subject routinely informed on himself? And to aggravate matters—beyond the apparent freedom I enjoyed—my father was a cool guy. He might offer my friends a Michelob. He might let them drive his Porsche around the block, snap a shot with the Hasselblad, tinker with his super-advanced Pioneer stereo system.

As my friends and I shot baskets in the driveway, my father would roar in from the tennis club blaring a song from *Nashville Skyline*, maybe "Lay Lady Lay" or "Girl from the North Country." He loved that beautiful, almost country record Bob Dylan made with Johnny Cash. But I had the other Dylan—the not-so-pretty-voiced prophet of End-Times divination who rattled through songs like "The Times They Are A-Changin'," "Hard Rain," and "It's All Over Now, Baby Blue." To my father, Dylan was just another singer, another Johnny Mathis or Frank Sinatra; to me, he was the very sound of deliverance, the rising summons of apocalypse, whose words would someday empty out the emptiness, wash this whole fake place away.

I went to the University of Virginia. I did well. I was cocaptain of the tennis team and a decent major college player—All-Atlantic Coast Conference my last year.

I went to law school and hated it. In both going and staying, I was probably trying to please my father.

And weirdly, instead of Torts and Trusts and Property and Contracts—rather than the black-letter rules I should have been stuffing into my brain—I began to have a different kind of thought. A repetitive thought. A couple hundred times a day, like a ticker tape running across the inside of my skull, I'd say this to myself: "I wonder how the world's going to end."

"I wonder how the world's going to end."

"I wonder how the world's going to end."

Now, the subject matter didn't really surprise me—I'd

always been drawn to apocalyptic-type things, beginning with my father's floodwaters and those loaded B-47 Stratojets—but the step into full-blown obsession was a first for me.

I don't really know what brought on the loop. It was before the R.E.M. song with the great refrain: "It's the end of the world as we know it . . . and I feel fine"; it was long after I'd read William Faulkner's Nobel Prize address about "the end of man," which my parents had framed in the basement next to the pool table; and though it was concurrent with the Strategic Air Command's production of Reagan's Peacekeeper MX missile, I don't recall any special fixation about that bomb.

Instead, I think I wanted to feel something in my body. The silent sound repeating. Like a heartbeat. A slowing down.

It still hadn't occurred to me that I didn't love my father.

11

~

I HAD NOT BEEN THERE when my father was exhumed. I had not attended his exhumation "party." And looking back maybe that was a mistake. Sure, it was a weird idea on my mother's part—to unearth my father after so many years—but in not supporting her weirdness, her call for ritual, I became haunted by the images I didn't see.

The backhoe at its digging and devouring.

Red clay opening beneath October trees.

A muddy coffin lifted from dark to light.

And not the scattered clumps of disturbed flowers I've talked about—not Queen Anne's lace or sweet everlasting, not horrible thistle or passionflower, not the flowers I'd search for years later along the road in ditches or in that plowed-under field at the Tri-State Crematory. I pictured, instead, the daisies and roses left on more recent graves and the wild oaks changing color around the cemetery edge.

Unfortunately, the uncomfortable event grew more

unsettling without ritual attention. I felt restless and agitated, thinking a little too much about what had happened to my father's body. I couldn't help it; the picture seemed at once so supernatural *and* real—a new twist on all those old vegetation myths about the changing seasons, death and rebirth, played out by the traveling bones of my father.

After a while, in the most peculiar manifestation of untended guilt, I even took my father's place in the cold ground. Though an embarrassing admission in its own right, this identification would prefigure more such embodiments with Tri-State. And the phenomenon began without warning, the mirroring generally occurring when I couldn't sleep, a common event for me in those days. Strangely, and with some alien comfort in my own bed, I'd catch myself imagining what it was like to be buried: days rocked by the slow shifting of continents, crust over hard mantle, deep shale sliding into an old rift valley. And breaking the peace of that state, the rumble of the backhoe coming. The clawing and tearing away from the earth. The changing into another thing.

For four days Lazarus lay in the cave, before Jesus said, "Come forth." And so my father arose, still wearing his seven-year grave clothes as he climbed from the ground. But unlike Lazarus, of course, my father did not walk away into the light of the New Testament. Rather, he was loaded onto a truck and taken to the Tri-State Crematory, where, with a gradually increasing number of rotting bodies, he would remain for five years.

I'd failed miserably to picture his flesh and bones when he'd first descended into that ground. I'd tried to bring myself to open the casket lid and look inside. But I couldn't do it. I was a coward.

And likewise, years later—almost casually, like it was a joke—I didn't go to see my father's corpse pulled from the grave. I didn't attend the ceremony planned for his exhumation. And I never made the link to my failed endeavor at this burial. I just didn't want to think about his lost body anymore; I was done.

And then my attempted suppression of the events entirely (and predictably) backfired. My imagination took over and my father's bizarre rebirth into death, his second death, took on a troubled new life.

When I first thought about the name "Tri-State" as it related to my father's death, I thought of that other vegetation myth's tripartite scheme; I thought of the Father, Son, and Holy Ghost. It seemed relevant in a way I couldn't figure out. But after a while I realized that the word had a different meaning beyond the obvious proximity of a Georgia crematory to the borders of Alabama and Tennessee. It also described another state of being, a kind of purgatory.

When my father was buried and then raised up into his second death, he really did enter a third state: the plane of restlessness that haunts the road between life and death. Tri-State.

Regarding that now-mythic field, I wondered what my father would think of the picture I carried with me. It didn't show much. Razed ground and some trees. Tread marks of a backhoe or other big machine. But certain aspects seemed prettily arranged. The sky, for example, catching streaks of cirrus and a few heavier puffs above the leaf line. Or the strange limb shadows of hidden trees that edged into the bottom of the scene, where the photographer must have stood in shade. Though just a quick snapshot, the photograph had power, I thought: It documented what happened while also capturing an eerie atmosphere of blight and vacancy.

And even the best photographer couldn't show what wasn't there, or what was there but couldn't be seen. I knew for a fact the bones of the dead lay scattered in bits and pieces just below that scoured dirt. I knew because I'd read all about it.

Just after the end of the official cleanup in 2002, the defense attorney for Brent Marsh invited a group of plaintiffs' lawyers to walk the still-wooded crematory grounds. As the *Atlanta Journal-Constitution* explained, the visit was supposed to be a "goodwill gesture" to provide the attorneys with a better feel for the place. It did. According to Brent Marsh's lawyer, the group found "several hundred human remains, small bone pieces, some large ones just lying around on the ground." The county director of emergency services compared it to a Civil War battlefield; indeed, the bloody battle of Chickamauga had been fought only a few miles away, and there fragments of bones and other relics are still regularly unearthed today. So it made sense that this modern field—where Brent Marsh recently had cast so many bodies—would hold hundreds of pieces of bone, locked in the ground like the seeds of wild grasses. In the end it was this afterimage, not the cleared field, that told more of what had happened there.

12

~~~

THERE ARE SOME STORIES you tell so often, or have lived so intensely, that they slow down. You can call up sensory details and rewind them with great vividness and imaginative accuracy—the difference between a breeze and a slight wind, for example, or the multiple shadings of dark, as if in the process of recollection and collection you hold a pile of photographs to guide your words, little triggers of memory and feeling that lead the tale onward. And erased by that greater subtlety is the usual distinction between telling and remembering; the performance is blurred together, collapsed in a fissure of smooth space and time—a story in which events move more slowly toward a purer wreckage, an assemblage that, given a certain point of view, seems to take on an unlikely order.

Back in 2002, the question of what had languished in the black box on my mother's shelf those last five years would have to wait another day. It was agreed that my mother would take the box to a local funeral home in Santa Fe the next morning to obtain a professional opinion as to its contents. If the cremains clearly were not of human origin, we would consider what to do next.

As night came on, the rain—changeable only by degree in the Oregon winter—fell in soft drops against the porch roof. No doubt I was drinking a Pabst Blue Ribbon, my drink of choice in the Portland days. In that town people used the weather as an excuse to drink too much, the sky always low and close.

I remember talking about my father with my wife, Kate, and how particularly strange it would be for his body to have ended up at Tri-State. Already his coming and going from this world involved a dramatic event, a dislocation of mock-biblical proportion: deluge, disinterment, and now—perhaps—resurrection.

Heads spinning with Scripture, we decided to walk down the hill for another drink.

At La Cruda, our neighborhood bar on Clinton Street, the light was too bright, the thirdhand tables precarious, the bathrooms frothy swamps. But it had become the place to go in the city because of the jukebox. The yellow beer remained a further attraction—"yellow" to distinguish it from the expensive microbrews offered at other bars—although its chief attraction was that it sold for a dollar a can.

Locals of all kinds floated through. Mostly people in bands, people who wanted to be in bands, people who wanted to date people in bands. And intermingled with these customers were older writers and artists, waiters and coffee shop workers. Typically everyone smoked and drank too much, arguing too long about some arcane point of rock 'n' roll history: "The most influential artist of the '70s *and* '80s? Definitely Alex Chilton . . . from power-pop to demented '50s trash rock . . ."

And always a core group of patrons had the best seats along the bar. These faithful were not there for the scene or for the music, at least that was not their primary motivation. They were there to drink. And they conducted their chosen ritual with a certain zeal, commencing every day in the afternoon and continuing beyond last call. I had known these people for a few years, but I could never maintain their fervor. They were all on the same mission. They had all come to this earth to sacrifice their bodies.

That night I was intent on keeping up with them. It was one thing to hear the Tri-State story on television. It was quite another to hear myself telling it from a new position.

"In the pines, maybe . . . maybe locked underwater in a vault."

As the night wore on—and as I told the story over and over—the image of my father's lost body became increasingly vivid, while my own limbs felt less necessary, less important.

"I'll find out tomorrow"—I heard my faraway voice say—"we're having the box checked to see if it's human."

Eventually Kate got a ride home, and I stayed for an after-hours drink with the devoted. It was at this time of night when the hardest drinkers began downing mind erasers—a three-layered cocktail consisting of vodka, Kahlua, and soda. The soda was supposed to "oxidize" the alcohol more quickly into your system, an explanation that always seemed unlikely to me. But I did like the name, which the faithful found useful. If they could just empty their minds as they emptied their glasses, the overall program of ruination would be that much easier.

My problem, however, was that the more I drank, the clearer my mind became. Or so it felt. On my occasional instances of real drunkenness, I was known to hold forth on numerous subjects, most typically my apocalyptic vision of things in which we humans, a marauding species hell-bent on devastating the world, would get what was coming to us. (This was a far cry from the finer points of rock 'n' roll usually discussed at the bar and reflected, instead, my extended history of such imaginings, from floods to bombs to that obsessive thought from law school.) And I had a long list of grievances—the present-day holocaust of species; the modern holocaust of the Jews and Gypsies and homosexuals; the past genocide, beginning with de Soto, of Native Americans. Like a child practicing scales on a piano, I drew from a list that went on and on, up and down, backward and forward through our ignoble history. And in retribution for these sins, we humans would receive a well-deserved apocalypse by way of global warming, nuclear obliteration, plague, etc., etc. (my list here being also quite long). "Something is coming," I'd say, my voice tightening with dread.

And yet if I stayed just a little later, as I did this night, these fire-and-brimstone sermons predictably broke down into crying. The faithful knew me well enough over the years to expect this. They knew I was a weeper. I'd put my arm around someone and the tears would just fall. I was crying for the sadness in the world—the great love I saw and felt for everyone and everything. I was crying for the absurdity of existence, the suffering as well as the beauty. All those things wrapped together, mixed in with another mind eraser. Sure, maudlin, but it was the End-Times— a topic the faithful knew something about. And when I walked home up the hill, the rain sliding from the sky, I heard myself crying for what was already gone.

13

~~~

I WONDERED WHAT I WOULD SAY if I had to nail my thoughts to a roadside pine. I decided my own sheets would have to be blank at this stage of my travels, just fluttering white ghosts fastened to wood. Or maybe I'd hammer that picture of the razed field at the Tri-State Crematory every few miles along my trail. Maybe that was my personal revelation. Because I did think I was onto something here. The pieces of bone and the pieces of lives. The hundreds of fragments and the thousands of photographs. Everything hidden and locked away. And there was some connection to the pictures themselves, the stolen moments in time, and my father's heavy overinvestment of parental capital in me. There was something revelatory about his fractured approach to both of these things.

On the west side of the road, I saw another Confederate Battle Flag standing weirdly alone in a small mowed field of ragged grass, and a sign below that read LT. COLONEL WILLIAM A. HEWLETT CAMP, SONS OF CONFEDERATE

VETERANS, JASPER ALABAMA. I supposed the flag marked the local chapter of the Southern "heritage" group, a not-so-innocuous organization still active in these parts. Surrounded by suffocating sheets of kudzu over pines, the dirty white pole and cheap sign looked tawdry and vacant.

Entering the outskirts of the old coal town, I passed through a poor black enclave not so removed from a Walker Evans photograph. A paint-peeled boardinghouse with a rickety balcony stood down a side road. Men sat in rusted chairs on dilapidated front porches. Children played in a ditch with sticks, poking at some small yellow flowers I didn't know. Black folks and white folks lined up at Bayou Fresh Seafood & Deli. More trucks pulled in for lunch.

My father had grown up poor. His father worked in the oil fields. And given the chance like so many others in the 1950s, he'd wagered everything on a utopian corporate vista that the world waved in front of him; he'd bought in completely. And urged on by those phony advertisements of that period, with their promise of accumulated horizon, he thought he'd feel better with a wife, two kids, two cars, a big house, a big yard, a big TV, four tennis rackets, ten suits, custom golf clubs, a Leica, a Hasselblad, and a Nikon. He thought he'd be happy in his sought-after managerial job that transferred him all over the country, uprooting him from where he was born and landing him in a dredged and gouged suburb in Atlanta. But when he wasn't, and when he still had to play like he was, simply because he'd bet the farm, bet his life and our lives, it fueled a simmering disturbance. And this was a guy who seemed destined for upheaval from the beginning, when that smooth water drowned his first home. This was a guy whom fate (dressed up as the Shit Fairy) had marked for special and afflicted treatment, whose bones would later lie muddled in a blighted place, where honeysuckle and thistles bloomed seasonally along the banks of a fake lake.

14

FOR THOSE WITHOUT SPANISH, the bar's name, La Cruda, means "the hangover." And I had a big one. After staggering drunkenly home up that Portland hill, I woke to find myself fully dressed on the bed, clothes radiating cigarette smoke. Rain fell heavily outside. And where I lay, images rose thickly from the exalted sadness of the previous evening. All those tears, I thought, and shook my head.

As I slipped back safely into dream, another image split the dark: a pile of skeletons drowned in a narrow vault. When I opened my eyes to drab noon and stumbled to find a phone, a distant voice spoke from the message machine, a voice I could hardly recognize. My mother was crying a cold and muffled cry. And though I couldn't decipher her words, I knew what they meant. My father was nowhere to be found in that black box on the shelf, the one she had talked to every day for five years.

The mind erasers had prepared me for this moment. At the bar, as I told my story, I had come to believe that he was at Tri-State, my story sounding more true with every drink. Eventually that truth provided a point of embarkation for my tumbling sadness.

But why him? I could think only of the lake and his five long years underwater. I was sure that's where he'd be—if there was any sense to this universe, his bones would be locked underwater.

My mother's phone was busy. My sister in Houston picked up on the first ring. "Can you fucking believe it?" she said. My mother always said with a mix of pride and horror that my sister had a sailor's mouth.

My sister went on to explain that the funeral director in Santa Fe had looked at the remains and decided they consisted mostly of concrete dust. Maybe a few bone fragments, but those appeared to be animal bone. Squirrel or dog. Nothing human.

We commiserated for a while about the situation, describing a range of emotions from outrage to disbelief.

"At least he was already dead," I said, meaning not recently alive when he arrived at Tri-State, meaning the exhumation. A flurry of small darts flew hard against my skull.

We laughed about that, but it wasn't a real laugh. We agreed we had two goals. The first was to calm down our mother, who my sister said had sounded pretty hysterical on the phone. Our mother had dug him up and now she would blame herself for what had happened to him at Tri-State. Plus, she had talked to that stupid box for a bunch of years, a box of nothing.

The second goal was to find our father's body.

15

⌇

HICKORYLAND BAR-B-QUE STEAK HOUSE, some old clothing and furniture shops with vintage storefronts, and, along the town square, hanging baskets filled with various flowers. This was the old downtown of Jasper. Unlike Tuscaloosa, where half the downtown was being leveled in the name of "revitalization," Jasper appeared to offer an almost quaint Southern setting—most of its old brick buildings intact from a hundred years ago.

Having located a parking place next to the looming Walker County Courthouse, I covered my flag with a half-open map of Alabama. Then I strolled toward the veterans' monument I'd seen on the corner. As in Tuscaloosa, the names of soldiers killed in battle from World War I to Vietnam were engraved on a series of marble tablets. Resting on one tablet, a small American flag extended from a wreath of red, white, and blue plastic flowers. This patriotic all-weather wreath was the kind placed on graves, while the flag was of the medium-size cloth variety people waved in parades.

And then front and center on the town square—as if waiting in ambush—a Confederate soldier abruptly stood above me on a tall pillar. Two more soldiers waited at the base of the stone-and-marble monument, flanked by the word COMRADES chiseled in bold letters. And sure enough, on a green wire easel in front of the monument, someone had placed a Confederate Battle Flag made out of the same plastic material as that red, white, and blue wreath stationed nearby.

I couldn't help but focus intently on the official sign attached to the carved slab—commemorating the dead remained a strong impulse for most people, as I knew only too well.

> The Confederate Monument was erected on November 13, 1907 and dedicated May 2, 1908 by the Jasper Chapter No. 925, United Daughters of the Confederacy, under the leadership of Elizabeth Cain Musgrove to honor the 1900 soldiers who served from Walker County. This monument was placed on the Alabama Register of Landmarks and Heritage May 19, 1999 by the Elizabeth Cain Musgrove Chapter No. 1929, UDC.

Unlike the Southern Baptists who actually promoted racism for so long, the United Daughters of the Confederacy was an ostensibly nonracist organization whose policies resulted in a great deal of racial strife. The group expressly

functioned as a Southern white women's "heritage" organization, whose primary actions involved the preserving
and erecting of Confederate monuments throughout the
region. But I also knew it had another mission—to pro-
mote a "truthful history of the War Between the States."
Since its inception in 1894, this meant, for example, making sure school textbooks offered a sympathetic view of
Southern history and that local cultural events always did
the same. Among the claims of this "truthful history" was
the insidious position that Confederate soldiers were simply fighting to protect "states' rights"—hence the insistence
on referring to the war as the War Between the States—
and not to preserve the institution of slavery.

It was clear, however, that "heritage" rather than history drove the UDC program. This genteel organization
of Southern ladies had little use for the reality of documented human suffering. In 1989, for instance, the group's
official magazine ran an article whitewashing the torments
of slave ships, claiming that sixteen inches of allotted deck
space per slave wasn't really so bad, given that more area
opened up quickly due to passenger deaths. At all costs
the organization strove to honor the bravery and commit-
ment of the Confederate soldiers, even at the price of ig-
noring the evils of slavery.

From the perspective of the UDC, as well as the less
genteel Sons of Confederate Veterans, it was the North
that had desecrated the South during the Civil War. The
body of the South had not only been defeated, supine on

the battlefield, but had also been dragged around and abused like Hector's corpse at Troy. As a first example, they would point to the flames of Atlanta and General Sherman's incendiary march to the sea. Hence the monuments and attempts to heal. Hence the bitterness and lack of remorse. And it didn't help matters that the honor code once so dominant in the Old South—a creed drawn from classical thought and mores, especially the valorous elements of Marcus Aurelius's stoicism—still echoed throughout the region. Some Southerners experienced any federal activity related to that original disgrace as a fresh violation of that code, from Reconstruction to civil rights to contemporary implementation of the Voting Rights Act. In the South, desecration was intensely tied to dishonor. Disturbed ground and disturbed integrity.

Not only did Achilles viciously transgress the warrior code in his treatment of Hector, but he also wanted his opponent's body devoured by "dogs and vultures"—a primal fear of classical culture. This wasn't just about the rotting and tearing of expired flesh. The Greeks believed that the stage between death and burial—that in-between threshold of travel—required great diligence by the living in the form of ritual and interment. Only with this care could the dead make their way into Hades. Otherwise, an abandoned and unritualized body remained doomed to roam the banks of the River Styx, a shade with a name but no passage. Thus Priam begged Achilles for the body of Hector. Thus the ghost of Patroclus entreated Achilles to bury him. Elpenor pleaded with Aeneas. And later on Antigone brashly buried the discarded body of her brother, Polynices, after it was decreed by Creon that the corpse be left to the animals and wind, "a feast for birds and dogs."

In an obvious and to me dishonorable act of omission, and like Achilles himself, the most devout practitioners of that Southern code of honor blatantly failed to identify their own desecrations. Though I didn't expect a more democratic tribute—I wasn't insane—it was still logical to note the absence from this "truthful history" of any monuments acknowledging the names of Indians driven from their land, or the names of black people shackled by slavery. There were no inscriptions recognizing those lynched in the Jim Crow era or the civil rights workers killed in their later struggle. Many homegrown acts of murder and humiliation were simply ignored, an inherent blindness of the code that originally proved disastrous for the South. And yet the system still held such power that only after a fierce existential struggle could a relative "Southern liberal" like Walker Percy—often held up as an intellectual conscience of the place—as well as his character Binx Bolling in *The Moviegoer*, repudiate the creed fifty years ago, and then only in its most ruinous aspects.

Swiftly glancing around with my cheap digital camera, a machine that would have held no place among my father's collection of high-quality equipment, I framed an artless snapshot of the Confederate flag and headed back to the car. Inside, I drew the Alabama map away and playfully pointed the viewer at the flag case.

But my bemusement widened to surprise when a strange commingling of images reflected back from the case: the Stars and Stripes, the Confederate Battle Flag with soldiers, a camera, a photograph, and me. The effect was hallucinogenic and the too-quick reality fracture suggested more breakage to come. Here I was, in my sudden corridor of collapsed meaning—the dislocated son of a dislocated father—floating above a plastic battle flag and soldiers that together hovered over a disarranged and thus dishonored American flag. For a few moments I drifted inside that image, or images, bewildered at my point of reference. If only I'd carried two (or three) cameras around like my father, I could have clicked the chorus of images together, holding a machine in each hand.

As careful excavation of ancient settlements has shown, the Cherokees once buried their relatives with an assortment of gifts for the afterlife, including shell beads, pendants, rattles, and clay pipes. If I could ever open that lid to my father's coffin—return to the scene of my failure and reverse my playing dead in the ground—I'd leave him that picture for his travels, the one I didn't have.

16

~~~

WITH THE NEWS that her box contained no sign of her husband, my mother was in bad shape. Sometimes crying. Sometimes waxing philosophical. Sometimes yelling loudly into the receiver.

"It's the Shit Fairy again," she complained with conviction. Now that she lived in Santa Fe, she always wore at least five turquoise rings and one Southwestern Indian necklace around town. Yet my mother was tough underneath all that style—a worthy adversary even for the Shit Fairy. She remained clearheaded about finding my father's body.

She stayed closely in touch with the Georgia Emergency Management Agency, which worked in tandem with the Georgia Bureau of Investigation and the state medical examiner's office to identify the bodies. Over the next few days, from conversations with the people on the ground as well as our own online investigations, we learned that we had a potential problem—actually several looming difficulties—in locating my father's body.

The main problem stemmed from the fact that my father had been embalmed and buried twelve years before. The embalming process eradicates some genetic markers, thereby reducing the chances of matching DNA from family members. Not that it would be impossible to identify an embalmed body through DNA, simply less likely.

Exposure to the elements also diminished the possibility of a DNA match. Not only had my father been embalmed and buried for seven years, but he had been raised from the dead and discarded at Tri-State for another five.

Finally, we understood that it might be harder to identify those bodies whose remains had been commingled in pits and vaults. At this point, we knew that several metal vaults had been found in the bushes, piled high with bodies, and that more pits had been discovered stuffed with many more corpses. Over the years, the putrefaction may have transferred DNA from one body to another, contaminating and possibly precluding a genetic identification of a particular corpse. It was a gruesome image, flesh melting into flesh. And if my father lay underwater in such a vault, the prospects of a match diminished even further.

As the author of our ill fortune, and our tormentor by way of overwrought biblical allusions, would the Shit Fairy pass up these opportunities? Could the Shit Fairy forgo another shot at Lazarus, Job, and the Flood?

Shit Fairy or not, we had to face up to the fact that the authorities would not retrieve viable DNA samples from all the bodies scattered and abandoned at Tri-State. We had to hope it didn't go that far. We had to hope that some identifying physical or circumstantial evidence—which the medical examiner's office now asked for—would lead to his discovery.

At this basic level of inquiry, however, we had factors going both ways. My father had no broken bones, no prosthetic devices that might distinguish him. On the other hand, he had died nearly twelve years before, theoretically making his state of decay more advanced than the newly deposited bodies at Tri-State. Generally, it takes nature about twelve years to transform an unembalmed body six feet under into a skeleton, depending on the climate and soil composition. The embalming helps to preserve the flesh, but the quality of that procedure varies dramatically from mortician to mortician. Yet the five years of exposure at Tri-State would hasten decay, the rate again determined by his exact location. And then there was the exhumation: He had arrived in his casket, whereas most other bodies would have shown up in body bags. We had heard reports that a few corpses still lay in their caskets in the woods. Would the Shit Fairy be so hospitable?

Finally, they asked about his clothes, which seemed strange to us—as if any mortal garment might withstand twelve years of putrefaction. My mother, however, remembered exactly what he had on. A plaid shirt and chinos, a brown sport coat to dress him up for the grave, and new custom-made cowboy boots.

As my mother told the story, several weeks before my father fell ill they had traveled to Santa Fe, where my father, unbeknownst to my mother, purchased a pair of $800 cowboy boots. True, they were individually made to fit his feet, and they had his name inscribed inside the heel, but $800! Now retired from IBM, he needed to begin practicing frugality, my mother complained.

I guess they had quite a row about that, an unusual occurrence for them, and my mother still felt a little guilty about it. Hell, she said, how was she to know he'd be dead within a few months? Anyway, because rigor mortis had set in, the funeral home had trouble getting those boots on, so, with my mother's blessing, they had slit the backs and pried his cold feet inside.

By Tuesday, February 26, the body count at Tri-State had risen dramatically to over three hundred, and another deeper, wetter pit had been found. The local authorities kept raising the number of charges against Brent Marsh, the alchemical operator of the crematory, who still remained in the Walker County Jail with bond set at $100,000. And there was still no word on my father's whereabouts.

It was a good night for another foray into smoke, drink, and rain. Again I set out for La Cruda. As it happens, however, I remember very little about that night, whether mind erasers were imbibed or not, whether I rose to those strained heights of drunken clarity. I don't even recall whether I did my crying jag before the faithful at the conclusion of the evening. No after-glimpse of comradeship, apocalyptic rantings, or the beauty of the walk home. Nothing about the particulars of the rain.

But I do recall waking late again, and again hearing the indecipherable choked crying of my mother on the answering machine, and again calling my sister for the story.

They found him in his coffin in the woods, not too far from the main crematory building.

The lid was on the coffin and the body was dry.

They found him because the Shit Fairy had chosen to sit this one out. And because those well-made custom cowboy boots still had my father's name written clearly in one heel.

Part Two

17

~~~

MY APOCALYPSE BEGAN WITH WATER, I'm pretty sure of that.

Somewhere in my child's brain, when I was still going to Sunday school and learning about the Bible, I heard about the Great Flood and mixed it up with my father. God would choose someone, just a regular person like Noah or Daddy, and have him build a big boat called an Ark. The rest of the people had done something wrong called Sin—a vague thing related to hitting or biting another child—and God was angry. Very angry. You should not bite or hit other people (or your dog) so that they fall down. God had picked Daddy because he liked to hammer, but Daddy didn't build a boat and then the rain came and the bulldozers came and the water rose so high over his farm that Daddy forgot to tell the local animals. So they died and we only had a car and Noah sent out a raven and we moved to Missouri and later that day the sun came out.

And goddammit . . . (it was a word my father said when he was angry). And goddammit God promised—like I promised not to lie about peeing outside—that he wouldn't do it again. God vowed with his big Pledge of Allegiance hand held high that the waters wouldn't rise again but then he *did* flood Daddy's farm and so God was very strong but sort of a liar.

Something like that.

I grew up thinking about water. About apocalypse. It made some sense. The Russians did have a zillion warheads pointed at us and we at them and of course my father did fly those big bombs over the Atlantic Ocean. (Was that why God flooded his first home?)

And some people, more particularly our neighbors, kept water in their bomb shelters, but we never had a bomb shelter so we were out of luck. (Was that why we kept moving around so much, to get away from the bombs? Was it a grown-up version of hide-and-seek?)

And in a related apocalypse, I wondered if I'd wake up one day and find everyone jabbering in a different language called Babel. The tower was called Babel, too, and I figured the big end-of-the-world-type missiles would stand about that tall. Unfortunately, in Babel-land, it would be impossible to knock on someone's bomb shelter and ask for a glass of water or a drink from their hose—because even if they answered they wouldn't know what you were talking about. (Was that why cereal boxes and comic books advertised that ubiquitous magic decoder ring on the back, an instrument of translation which, if held high enough in the air on a closed fist, pulled bits of intelligible information from the neighbors' gibberish-smacking mouths?)

And that was another thing, speaking of comic books, supposedly only Jesus could walk on water, but couldn't Superman do that, too? I mean the guy could spin the whole world backward if he wanted to—which made it *yesterday*—a feat that would also be helpful if the world happened to end and you needed another day to make things right. But then if Superman could make it yesterday, couldn't he also take a simple stroll across a stretch of water? Across a lake? Across my father's pastures and fields sunk fathoms below?

Obviously, there was a lot to worry about. Though other kids didn't seem so worried.

My sister laughed at me when I explained how, at bedtime, I'd casually asked God if it would rain the next day and he said no from my dark closet. If the answer had been yes, his deep voice bellowing from behind a rack of small coats, then I guess I would have asked about the weather for the next thirty-nine days.

Water.

And I never heard any playground talk about apocalypse, not a peep. Though I, inclined to research, pulled the family Bible from the shelf next to the row of *World Book Encyclopedia* and studied Revelation for some kind of clue. At the time I was terrifically afraid of that book of the Bible and could suffer only a few minutes of scouring the text, but over a period I gathered the basic idea. Blood rained from the sky and the sea turned to blood and all the creatures in the sea drowned in blood. One angel poured his vial of wrath into the rivers and they became blood, too. And a star called Wormwood (doubly scary for me given my mother's morbid fear of death accompanied with worms) fell into the water and everyone, including all the animals, died from drinking more blood.

Of course, this was all in conjunction with me playing the flood game in the backyard, imagining the black clouds of dust and rain approaching and then running indoors gasping—my young mind just a step ahead of the rising waters.

Daddy. God. Missiles. Blood. Babel. Water.

It was quite a burden for a small child, one that I bore silently and alone.

And when as a teenager I finally arrived in my suburban Atlanta dead ends, my emerging rational self began to sort through these disturbing images, eventually discarding the idea of a literal God while translating the Great Flood into personal myth. As for Revelation, I soon managed to elevate its terror into high metaphor (the miraculous concept of metaphor acquired, I believe, from my tenth-grade Southern literature class featuring homegrown critics of the South such as Faulkner, O'Connor, and Lee), and suddenly I could build my own apocalypse from a wealth of real-world events. Not only did I pick up waves of a Confederate American nothingness from my invisible inner decoder as I prowled around the dug-out cul-de-sacs and half-built houses, I also received news, mostly from TV, of impending doom. Air pollution. Water pollution. Oil slicks and ozone holes. Rain forests—especially the one surrounding that giant serpent-shaped river called the Amazon—bulldozed and burned away, slashed and gouged. Radiation and chemicals and dead children. Creatures, like the dinosaurs of sixty-five million years ago, rapidly disappearing from the world as humans blindly dredged and paved, dredged and paved.

And then how strange to cast these charged images of destruction against the nothingness of my vagabond corporate childhood, against the nothingness of my father's inscribed life. How strange to sense something more than pure blankness, more than just a wind of zeros assaulting the air.

In fact, by the time I left those desperate dead ends for college, everything around me appeared both empty *and* wrong. Not only was the suburban life alienating, but it was also the input and output, engine and product, of a runaway corporate capitalism—yes, I was beginning to get the lingo down—whose international machinations functioned as a catalyst for our new apocalypse. Of course I couldn't neatly hook up all the causal factors for every strand of approaching destruction directly to my father, or to IBM, but I could try, and in the mid-1970s I could begin to make sense of the rebellion of the past decade, its critique of materialism as bad for the good earth. These were still oversize ideas for a high school kid, bluntly categorized and wielded, but they began to take hold. And as shown in my occasional late-night diatribes in a Portland bar, these concepts would be crystallized and refined over the coming years.

So it was not surprising that apocalypse rode with me that day.

Originally, when I first approached the outskirts of Jasper, I wondered whether my father had also experienced an intimation of emptiness, a breach of nothingness deep down near those already disturbed plates of his own history. I wondered whether he'd vaguely sensed the meaninglessness of his own rampant materialism, as well as the culture's, and so embarked on his second career as amateur photographer . . . ultimately a twisted one of gadgets and machines, distorted into just another form of materialism because he never acknowledged the problem to himself. He could never quite escape the power of his early indoctrination.

Yet it was not until I exited the other side of Jasper on my pilgrimage day, the sun shining straight down, that I connected my predilection for End-Times to my father's pictures. Instead of angels pouring vials of blood into the waters of the world, I had my own kind of vision . . . the weird kind that occurred only in my head.

As I pulled back onto the highway, a hovering of just empty blue sky above my horizon, I imagined that each time my father took a photo of me, or anyone in my family going about some mundane suburban business, he was clicking another picture of the apocalypse.

18

DURING THE DAYS FOLLOWING the discovery of my father's body at Tri-State, my family went about the business of the dead. Initially, we made arrangements for my father's belated cremation, a thing done quickly and once more without ritual due to the exigencies of the circumstances. The Georgia Emergency Management Agency had possession of his body, and they needed to know what to do with it. A local funeral home took custody, and this time my mother received my father's actual cremains by a trusted friend's hand delivery.

Within this volatile period, we all had to find a place for the news. My family's collective response to the unfolding of events ranged across the emotional spectrum, with especially dramatic movements through horror, anger, and sadness. Again, we had no guidelines for such strangeness, no cultural markers for dealing with my father's second death. It was a disorienting time, in which we all had to construct a new way to mourn.

And soon we began to exhibit some individual tendencies. My sister appeared to focus particularly on the black comedy aspects of the situation—of which there were several, given the Gothic nature of the Tri-State Crematory Incident. Wasn't it a little weird, she asked, that no one noticed the piling up of hundreds of bodies not so far from a main road? Was this a regular kind of occurrence for the hill folk of north Georgia? And how could a stupid mixture of concrete dust and whatever fool everyone, including all those funeral directors, for five years? And then there was our own collective story about the boots, which, though ultimately disturbing and graphic, seemed scripted from a mock horror movie. Our father, she kept saying, "would have laughed his ass off about that one."

And in response to the often-expressed belief that the Tri-State victims somehow possessed "restless spirits," she proclaimed that when she died she wouldn't mind if her own corpse was left out in the woods.

"I don't fucking care," she announced. To her, in an expression of (unchristian) dualism, a body was just a body in death. It was a thing, disconnected forever from all but its thingness.

In fact, her response was so emphatic that I wondered if she might be a candidate for one of the body farms set up in various parts of the country. In such places scientists studied the effects of putrefaction on bodies intentionally left exposed under a variety of controlled circumstances, in order to enhance the knowledge of biology, pathology, and forensics. Ironically, people were doing the same thing that Brent Marsh had done—scattering dead bodies in dirt, leaves, and pits—but in a manner sanctioned by the culture and state. The only real difference lay in the purpose behind the endeavor, and, of course, that the bodies once belonged to willing volunteers. In retrospect, my sister's proclamation seemed a way to identify with her own father's discarded body. She declared her readiness to step into his shoes (or boots). It was a way to lessen the trauma of his desecration.

As for my mother, she began to express louder and more outlandish versions of guilt and regret. She was mad, too, calling Brent Marsh a variety of choice names.

"They ought to throw that Brent fella down a big hole himself," she yelled. "See how he likes it!"

Regarding her remorse at having precipitated the event, having unearthed my father's body from his first home in the ground, my sister and I tried to reassure her. Clearly the burial/worm phobia was a legitimate fear, and we'd both condoned the exhumation, even while choosing not to be present at it. Obviously she'd had no idea that her husband's body would end up at the Tri-State hellscape, lounging in the woods those long years.

And now my mother had the Shit Fairy. She could trace all her misfortune back to that personage, blaming it for everything from her own cancer to my father's premature death to his body's eventual stay at the crematory. Though she never experienced any real supernatural solace from the Shit Fairy, I believe its conjuring did provide some sideways comfort, some consolation in the very declaration of its blasphemous name. In other words, the deflection of trauma by the performance was real, even if the entity was not. And for her I think the Shit Fairy was essentially an expression of intelligent fate, an agnostic's funny entertainment of the notion that things happened for a reason. Though she was hard to pin down on these matters, I think she leaned in the direction of some kind of soft determinism. Certainly the boots story, which the Shit Fairy orchestrated and then ultimately sat out, had the synchronous ring of fate.

And finally there was me.

Beyond bewilderment and the gamut of expected emotions, I immediately had a big problem. On the one hand, I shared my sister's view that a body was just a body, a thing without any actual meaning after death except as a symbol of a person's life. I did not accept as true, for instance, that my father's shadow was troubled in the woods, haunting the banks of the Tri-State lake.

Instead I considered human beings as simply flesh animated by a chemical consciousness—a consciousness that immediately disappeared into nothingness upon death. I had no belief in the sacredness of the dead form, nor did I believe that a corpse housed any kind of ghost or spirit. A body was just a body was just a body . . . It was a conviction that entitled me to a limited reaction to the desecration—perhaps confusion, anger, and some feeling of violation, but not much more. Within the confines of my unadorned belief system, there just didn't seem to be room for a greater disturbance.

And yet I did have more in the way of trouble . . . picture trouble . . .

Essentially I couldn't get away from the images of Tri-State.

I couldn't stop seeing the landscape of bodies strewn about the crematory grounds, piled up in vaults and tossed together in mass graves, scattered among the old mattresses, bottles, and pallets like more trash. I couldn't stop imagining the eyes that were no longer eyes gazing up into an unconstellated firmament, where one day the angels would not pour down vials of wrath and blood because I didn't believe in angels. I didn't believe in that particular apocalypse. And I couldn't help seeing that damn pool table with its nest of scavenged limbs and leaves.

Strangely, these terrifying images were all fantasies— snapshots conjured by a fallow brain. Clearly no news organization, print or television, would offer graphic pictures or clips of decomposing bodies drawn from shallow pits or pried from old caskets. Such horrors were not fit for a general audience. Instead, I drew most of my images from the website of the *Atlanta Journal-Constitution*, which did not show much more in the way of pictures but revealed a great deal in the form of words. During those opening weeks, the reporter, Norman Arey, wrote in detail of the mass desecration, and using his descriptions as points of embarkation

I conjured images that I then filed away under Disturbed. Eventually, I translated his stories into an entire album of Tri-State Crematory photographs, which I pulled down regularly from an internal shelf.

Generally it worked like this: Arey would set a scene or describe a fact and I'd dress it up from there.

One such fact I embellished in my head was the ghastly image of the "vaults," which, I understood from Arey's articles, had been stuffed with numerous bodies. These five metal vaults were found in the large storage shed, stacked one on top of another. From his description I deduced that Brent Marsh had used a single-body burial vault to hold multiple corpses that he failed to cremate. Normally a vault was used as a grave liner to keep the casket dry and to prevent a shallow depression at the cemetery. But Brent Marsh, in his innovative use of the container, slung in a single corpse and, as the flesh putrefied and fluids evaporated, he had room for more corpses on top. Given organic matter's method of simplifying itself over time, he could then fill an individual vault with five or so "reduced" corpses, saving space for more bodies elsewhere.

So I had pictures like these accumulating in my head, a gruesome slide show of the collective dead.

And then, of course, I had more to deal with regarding my father himself.

Though I wasn't sure exactly where they'd found him, I knew his coffin had lain in the brush and trees not so far from the main crematory building. And I knew he'd been there for five years. So I wondered about his deadly state—his rate of molder and decay. Just how far gone were those feet lodged in his boots? Was he mummified or mostly bones? And was his face still recognizable, the face that so strongly resembled my own?

Obviously—somewhere in the teeming backwoods of my imagination—a body was not a body was not just bones.

And though I didn't exactly think of it at the time, I know I was afraid. I'd been pushed toward the edge of dread, the black hole of oblivion.

Without the protection of a supernatural belief, I was suddenly confronted with the finality of my father's death—his animal death and my own. With all ritual displaced by Brent Marsh's conjuring of alchemical concrete dust and bone, I was alone with death itself, as exposed as my father in the close woods. And I couldn't just concoct a belief in the spirit, soul, or afterlife, ideas I'd discarded long ago. I couldn't manufacture a faith in determinism—whether that offered by God, the Shit Fairy, or some guiding principle of the universe. In an excruciating way my body was too real, too transitory, and it was fading fast just like my father and those other fragile things left rotting at Tri-State.

And so it was, face-to-face with my father's dead self, with dread, I wondered what it was like—I wondered what it was like being dead. I thought of him and I thought of me. I thought of snakes crawling over and mice skittering through, coyotes gliding by and bees buzzing around. Stirring of body bags and murmur of lake, especially at night, with a little wind. And finally our eyes gazed together into a black casket sky that reflected the colors of a shifting world—red moving to yellow and back again to green.

My father came alive—well, not quite alive but animated—a thing that could feel his death through all the human senses. It was a simple way to displace the terror of my father's death—much like my sister's declaring her own body could be thrown into the woods—by identifying with his plight and becoming more dead myself. The gesture seemed natural and was possibly even normal to some extent.

But soon, as occurred with my excursion underground after his exhumation, the images grew uncomfortably close. I'd begotten a thing that could show me his death, allow me entrance into his discarded bones, his disappearing flesh—and too often I accepted his express invitations. These meetings began reactively and without premeditation, and then darkened with repetition.

Human beings are funny things. We go on small pilgrimages without knowing we are on them. We roam around in our daily lives and wish for something significant or special to happen. And then occasionally we embark on big pilgrimages that project an end point—a point that might be religious or spiritual, or in my case a razed and abandoned field in the north Georgia mountains.

But we need a lot of luck and we need to follow the signs. And so it was that during those first days of Tri-State I had made my arrangements. I'd sown the idea of my father, animated and engaged, rising from the unhappy earth. From the beginning, and perhaps hidden from view for his own protection, I'd endowed my father with the power of becoming—a thing that might bloom beautifully into himself. He was just the kind of ghost flower that might appear somewhere along my road.

19

〰

ALREADY I WAS LOOKING for him as I passed by Taco Bell, Holiday Inn and KFC, Papa John's and Wendy's and Au-toZone, Ruby Tuesday and CVS and Kmart and Wal-mart. In general I knew this was not the best habitat for real wildflowers, even of the disturbed variety, but maybe ghost flowers appeared anywhere—like those drowned shoal lilies along the Black Warrior River. The real blos-soms of these flowers, once the largest stand on earth, would never return to this world. They had no home be-neath that smooth-water postcard and fake lake, nowhere to go. But the ghost lilies had made it back. I'd seen their perfect white heads swaying clearly below the water when I considered turning down a county road just a couple of hours ago.

Jesus . . . in the core of me I felt a wave of depression every time I came across this part of America, which meant I must have been depressed quite a bit. I felt we'd traded the real flowers' home for another type of world.

We'd dammed and dredged and channelized and paved and leveled and killed—and now we mostly had locations like this left to experience, dumb malls and big-box stores where people bought meaningless products they were told to buy, rows of shopping carts beckoning from parking lots, drive-thru lines reeling in oversize trucks and cars like silly fish. Mindless jobs to service all that moving, transacting, and devouring, and then mindless products to distract people from those jobs. A devastating cycle of prescribed and disembodied consuming, processing, and production that appeared only to accelerate as our age went on.

Glancing across at my rumpled flag, I wondered why. Why me? Why did I see things this shadowed way? Decent people like my father, intelligent and good people, could drive through this stretch and see an entirely different picture. My father, for example, definitely would not have chosen to live or work around here, but he did like to consume in such places. He was always out for a bargain, even as he serviced his patriotic spending problem, and so would hit Kmart as likely as some high-end photography store. If questioned, he'd make the basic Adam Smith argument that commerce had a mind and intelligence of its own, which functioned fairly over time and more efficiently without government intrusion. And now, he'd say, commerce operated on a global scale, and opening up markets everywhere would help lift developing countries out of their extreme poverty. Didn't I believe children in

Africa deserved electricity and running water? In a more prosperous world, then, we'd be better able to tackle looming social and environmental problems. People had to eat before they saved someone else, much less a spotted owl or river mussel. And by the way, he'd say, all these folks out here were real people, too. Was I some kind of elitist? These were good working people, most of them kind people, who had houses and cars and families and children. And they were free to make their own choices about how to live their lives. Did I want to tell them how to exist in the world? Or maybe I just didn't like the way it looked, a boring line of block-shaped stores and malls. Maybe my argument was ultimately aesthetic?

Yet this was no time or place to engage my father in economic debate, especially when he still hadn't materialized beyond that plastic flag case. This was not a pilgrimage into the dismal science. Obviously I thought the foundations of his argument to be off the mark. But the more pressing and interesting question was why I felt like this. Not the sinking feeling at coming upon an ugly swath of American retail—I think a lot of people experience that now to varying degrees. It was completely normal among the people I knew, though I did appear to have an acute case. But the other feeling, the End-Times one, my recurring leap from here to apocalypse.

I supposed I might have the apocalypse gene: a predisposition to prophetic revelation and doomsday excitability. Just as the alcoholism gene floated out there in my family genetic waters, maybe the Last Days gene did, too. Nature and nurture. Maybe I was born with an inclination for cataclysmic thinking, drawn like gravity to those incantatory sentences of the Bible's last chapter, and then my life had pulled the trigger. A loaded gun, so to speak. For someone with the A gene, a childhood in the first-ever nuclear age coupled with impending signs of environmental collapse (global warming, species holocaust, etc.) certainly seemed enough to manifest the predisposition. And then on top of it, I'd personally experienced fantastic events of small apocalypse such as the drowning of my father's farm, my father's more recent rising from the dead like Lazarus—no, like the dead in Revelation!—and then all those bodies left rotting in the woods at the Tri-State Crematory.

Ahhh!—it was more like Revelation . . .

Of course my father's unburying had always made me think of Lazarus, Jesus calling forth the four-days-dead body, but really it was the End-Times resurrection that the exhumation more strongly resembled. A failed resurrection without redemption.

Not the Rapture—that was a nineteenth-century invention and most popularly conceived today as occurring before the seven-year Tribulation and emergence of the Antichrist—when all breathing born-again Christians would be yanked straight up to heaven. (Terrifically, as a kind of signing bonus, by this interpretation born-again Christians got a free pass from the unimaginable violence and horror of the Tribulation.) But by Revelation I meant the more traditional yet still literal version of that apocalypse—when Jesus would come again to fight the Battle of Armageddon and establish a thousand-year rule of God's Kingdom on earth. Upon his return, Jesus would raise the righteous dead in their "resurrected and glorified bodies" to dwell forever in eternal heaven. I loved that phrase, "resurrected and glorified bodies"—I'd seen it on the Southern Baptist Convention website.

Through the lens of the Second Coming, then, my father's exhumation could be seen as a prelude to that great uplifting, a failed test case, in which his *un*glorified body got resurrected only a little ways into the air, his casket door malfunctioned, his wings fizzled, and finally his still-putrefying body was dumped in the woods at the Tri-State Crematory. Too bad.

And so my self-revelation was at hand.

I had the A gene and then my life experiences had brought my apocalyptic predisposition to fruition. My switch turned on, I was always thinking about apocalypse in one way or another, or at least it simmered just below the surface. And that was the reason—thank you, Jesus!—a relatively benign length of American commercial real estate made me jump to End-Times thinking. Just as I had all along my pilgrimage, I sensed, in such places, signs of the Tribulation and called forth evidence of the evil that had led us into catastrophe.

I followed a logging truck as it turned off the commercial strip and pretty soon I was back in the country, still on Highway 69, whizzing by abandoned farmhouses and lived-in mobile homes, a few well-kept brick houses scattered here and there. The Tribulation was everywhere? Had I lost my mind? As if in answer, I passed two real signs (with real letters)—one signaling Smith Lake lay just ahead, a massive fake lake built not so long ago, and another advertising a house of worship called the Church of Reconciliation. A third reply came from the symbolic world—a clutch of those small yellow wildflowers I couldn't identify, lingering like hitchhikers by a roadside ditch.

What was this trip *really* about? On a certain level, I supposed my busy brain functioned like a good lawyer's brain, compiling and employing only the best evidence to push an argument—slavery and its hangover of longstanding prejudice, Native American genocide, religious bigotry, environmental ruin. These were all signs of my kind of Tribulation—an unsupernatural turmoil involving human violence and violence against the earth—culminating in my kind of apocalypse in which the world would be humanly undone either with a bang (most likely nuclear) or with a whimper (most likely climate change and its slower degradation). And though these threats were real—very real—mine was a selective version of history, a one-way parade leading always and only to the brink. In other words, I needed to feed that part of me, my addiction to cataclysm, and so I saw signs of the Tribulation everywhere. Everything was disturbed ground.

Another person, for example, could have embarked on my pilgrimage road and reported back somewhat less dire sightings: a downtown Tuscaloosa trying to reinvigorate itself by demolishing some decrepit buildings with rundown businesses; some Confederate Battle Flags, sure, but only a fraction of what flapped out there during the civil rights era; and then the land itself, torn up in spots but beyond those a lush landscape burgeoning with oaks and pines and a broad assortment of pretty wildflowers.

As I steadied my hands on the wheel, my mind wandered back around to de Soto, my fellow traveler in a different Age of Discovery, who himself had no map and whose exact path to this day remains blurred. Though there's clarity on the sequence of states—Florida, Georgia, South and North Carolina, Tennessee, Georgia again, Alabama, Mississippi, Arkansas, Texas, and then back to an escape route along the Mississippi River—the trail itself often fades away into the fields and swamps.

I had a clearer destination to the east, but now I wondered about that. And I wondered who I was without my obsession and predisposition, my apocalyptic way of seeing and being in the world.

Maybe I was simply converted, one of the blessedly born-again for whom the veil had been lifted. Or, even less desirable, maybe this was some kind of additional craziness I'd inherited along with the A gene. Just as Brent Marsh hoarded those bodies and stuffed them everywhere and anywhere he could, I likewise hoarded my Last Days pictures as I went along, gathering signs of the Tribulation as obsessively as he gathered bones. And then there was the other guy, my father. Didn't all three of us—the alchemical Brent Marsh, my father, and I—lead secret lives of disturbance? Weren't we all strange prophets of disorder? And, given all this, couldn't I raise my father up and make him alive, lift up his glorified flower body into a brilliant new raiment whose brighter glow would shine the way?

Wow, I *was* pretty fucking crazy. I shivered giddily. I felt the Shit Fairy's breath sliding coldly along my neck.

20

ᨠ

BY THE END of February 2002, local authorities had charged Brent Marsh with hundreds of counts of theft by deception and abuse of a corpse. He offered no statements about the case and appeared blank faced as police shuttled him back and forth to the courthouse. Rumors quickly filled the vacuum. A report surfaced that for years the crematory incinerator remained inoperable due to a bad timer, suggesting, as a primary cause of the desecration, that Brent Marsh had simply failed to order a replacement part since 1997. More elaborate accounts proposed that Brent Marsh practiced necrophilia, offering photographs of compromised corpses on the Internet. Some speculated he trafficked in body parts.

Acting swiftly, the Georgia Bureau of Investigation managed to dismiss these rumors, except the suggestion of a faulty incinerator. In fact the machine did fail to function when authorities descended upon Tri-State, but agents simply hotwired the defective timer and the burner switched on. And though no one knew the duration of the timer's malfunction, apparently Brent Marsh had also simply hotwired the mechanism when necessary. After all, the man had cremated some six-hundred-plus bodies during that same five-year period, and thus the bad timer had little or nothing to do with his dereliction of duty. We all waited for a better answer: family members and the public as well. Unfortunately, in a pattern that continued for years concerning the Tri-State Crematory Incident, a veil soon dropped over the evidence. In early March, to prevent jury prejudice and protect Brent Marsh's rights, the judge in the criminal case slapped a gag order on the proceedings, forbidding authorities from providing fresh information to the public. Legally it was a sound move. Suddenly, however, regarding the worst mass desecration in modern American history, a near blackout of important news occurred.

In short, the families knew only the approximate number of desecrated bodies (somewhere in the 330s) but nothing regarding the final count of unidentified bodies and had no information whatever as to how many bodies lay rotting together in pits or the particular number of corpses desecrated each year. And officially there was nothing— absolutely nothing—regarding Brent Marsh's state of mind.

It was during this time that I made the leap from Brent Marsh the crazy crematory operator to Brent Marsh the alchemist. On the one hand, I knew I'd never escape from Brent Marsh the crazy crematory operator, the sad and sordid figure who'd left my father's body outside for five long years. On the other hand, recast as an alchemist, a practitioner of an ancient art who strove to transmute base materials to a sacred substance, he offered some relief from the grisly circumstances.

Yet how was this connected to my penchant for tumult, my newly discovered tendency to foreground apocalypse in the day-to-day world?

I recalled stumbling across a precursor of Revelation, an early writing called *The Book of the Watchers*, composed by Jewish scribes in the third century BCE. To my surprise, a number of apocalypses existed outside the two included in the Bible, the Book of Daniel and Revelation, and in fact the apocalypse was a popular literary genre across the Holy Land. As told in some translations of *The Book of the Watchers*, copied and interpreted over the years, it was a cadre of fallen angels who taught humans the forbidden knowledge of alchemy, an esotericism intended for divine use only. It was a detail I'd noted with interest, given my proclivities, one that now seemed laden with heavy correspondence: Apocalypse and alchemy shared a mythic relation across the millennia.

Equally compelling, for alchemists, everything in nature existed upon a hierarchy of purification, with lead, copper, and silver simply stepped-down versions of gold. Thus in de Soto's age, it was accepted as "scientific" fact that depleted gold mines rejuvenated over time, grew more gold nuggets like living things. So an alchemist's job was to bring forth higher, more perfect fruit, hasten the process of nature, and ripen lead into silver and silver into gold. Again, at the time this seemed a matter of some interest, but now the images glowed with significance. Wasn't I attempting to summon my father's glorified body along the road, to bring forth his full flowering and raiment? And in my inclination to emphasize Tribulation-type events, wasn't I seeking the ever more perfect fruit of our reckoning?

And what about a recent theory offered by McCracken Poston, Brent Marsh's attorney, suggesting that mercury poisoning had contributed to, if not caused, his client's desecrating behavior? According to Poston, the contamination resulted from the incineration of old dental work in a poorly ventilated crematory building. In sum, Poston claimed that Brent Marsh was a "mad hatter."

Though dismissed by the state medical examiner as scientifically unsupported, the mad-hatter hypothesis was not unreasonable. A test-kit sample of Brent Marsh's hair had revealed suspiciously high levels of arsenic, aluminum, cadmium, lead, nickel, and tin—substances that were the very signature of mercury poisoning. Even the doubting examiner suggested further testing, an act that never occurred. Yet without scientific confirmation—as a primary cause, at least—the theory simply didn't hold up against the weight of evidence. The theory didn't explain how

Brent Marsh could act normally in the public arena—including serving on the board of the Walker County Division of Family and Children Services—if he suffered from a severe neurological disorder. Could one really be a mad hatter in only one aspect of life? It didn't seem possible to me.

Moreover, the theory failed to consider Brent Marsh's suspected hoarding disease, as well as his brilliantly analytical deceit in creating his alchemical mix of concrete dust and bones. Still, for all its inadequacies, Poston's theory did provide another layer of complexity to the question of Brent Marsh, to the underlying disturbance that haunted the man.

When Poston presented his theory, I immediately did my homework on mercury's connection to alchemy—whose practitioners, I should note, often trolled the symbolic pronouncements of Revelation for new formulas. And I found that mercury, known as quicksilver due to its color and semifluid state, obtained an exalted place in alchemy because of a most dramatic act: When it's combined with nitric acid, the chemical reaction produces a smoky red gas and red crystals. Mesmerized, alchemists came to consider quicksilver the key to transformation itself, transcending the basic dualisms of their cosmological reality: solid and liquid, death and life, heaven and earth.

For me, that magical experiment conjured first an image of hell (redness all around) and then my father laboring in the cloudy light of his darkroom, stirring his chemicals and eventually pulling my image—which uncannily mirrored his own—from a series of red-tinged baths . . . *whosoever was not found written in the book of life was cast into the lake of fire . . .*

And now—after everything—it was I who struggled to write my own version of apocalypse, suffused with symbolic sightings. It was I who had become something of a mad hatter on this day.

Through the cloudless light of northern Alabama, I swerved off Highway 69 and followed the way to Lewis Smith Lake, to view one of the hydroelectric dams up close. The steep terrain was a sign that swift river water once cascaded down these slopes. Today there was a road and a long metal fence belonging to the Alabama Power Company.

When I broke into the open, a red-tailed hawk drifted above a grassy field. An earthen dam stretched beyond. It was the largest such dam in the eastern United States, but it didn't look that big to me. Heavy gray stones buttressed the line and dark water lapped against it. A sign said DANGEROUS CURRENTS, though none were visible.

The lake was vacant and loud with wind.

From the boat launch tilting beneath me, I raised my camera and took a few quick shots: panorama of the earthen dam, a fancy house on the far bank, the deep water. I realized these were only the second photographs I'd taken on my trip, apart from the Velasquez-type metapicture of dueling flags and faces. In contrast, these images were almost empty, like pictures of the wind itself.

I didn't know the exact number of species that perished forever because of this particular dam—unlike the infamous Coosa River die-off about sixty miles southeast of here—but lost creatures were part of the deal. As if on cue, ugly and symbolical, two bony-faced vultures circled the parking lot. On the way out I stopped the car again to click a picture of a dead kite tangled in the power lines along the green field.

21

~~

WITH THE GAG ORDER STILL IN PLACE through the summer of 2002, no new information appeared about the specifics of the case, and as the shock receded, I began to think more closely about the plight of others beyond my family. In the most significant way, of course, our position was anomalous—my father had been dead for twelve years. Although I remained besieged by the images of Tri-State and my father's original digging-up, as well as my own apocalyptic imaginings, I was not racked with the sorrow of his immediate passing.

Like my mother, some families had received no human cremains at all, instead acquiring Brent Marsh's special mixture of concrete dust and bone. And although this sleight of hand left my mother distraught, angry, and perplexed, the distress was magnified for those who'd more recently experienced the loss of a loved one, some just a few weeks or months before the case broke open in February 2002. These poor people had to process not only a fresh death but also the added anxiety of a very fetid desecration—whether the bodies were rotting together in pits and burial vaults, or sprawled by one another in the tangled brush, exposed as prey for foraging animals.

Yet within this group who received fake cremains, a smaller group experienced an even greater affliction. Some families, devastatingly, had failed to find a body at all. This meant either another party (or parties) had received the family member's cremains, or the body could not be identified because of its degraded state—a sad commingling of flesh, bone, and DNA. Again, with the blackout on information, the number of such frustrated families remained a mystery, though their suffering was clear: They had lost both a loved one and that loved one's body; no earthly connection remained to the living past.

Finally, during the five-year period of the Tri-State Crematory Incident, Brent Marsh sent 660 families a collection of human cremains. At first glance one would think these people were spared the horror of desecration, but obviously these husbands and wives and children and grandchildren had to think twice about the cremains they'd solemnly scattered, or placed in a vase on a shelf somewhere. Recall that DNA does not survive cremation. Add to this fact the strong suspicion that Brent Marsh had neither carefully nor individually burned the bodies he'd managed to cremate. In sum, these families lived in the unsettled state of not knowing whose cremains they'd obtained—whether relative, stranger, or some combination thereof.

And if a complete stranger, then the possibility always existed that the loved one's body remained unidentified and undeciphered among the blended names of decay. Inevitably these people had a different question: Whose ashes and whose dust?

And within all these groups, the questions of ashes and dust and flesh and bone registered different intensities on the disturbance scale. Within my own family, for example, we ranged from the mildly agitated (my sister's indifference to the idea of her own corpse left in the woods) to the strongly afflicted (my mother's struggle through a broad palette of torments) to the obsessively disarranged (my irreligious descent into End-Times putrescence). But what about the more religiously inclined victim-families? Even though cremation remained disfavored among conservative Christian groups, my guess was that at least two-thirds of the affected families in this rural corner of the Deep South would identify as evangelicals, with the figure possibly even higher due to the region's dearth of Catholics and lapsed Protestants. But this certainly didn't dictate a prescribed emotional response.

On the one hand, it was true that evangelical Christians tend to embrace the solace of design, imputing the desecration to God's overall plan. For these faithful, everything happened for a reason. Your crappy job at Walmart happened for a reason, your divorce happened for a reason, the 9/11 attacks happened for a reason, etc. Consolation also lay in the knowledge that the dead (assuming a personal relationship with Jesus themselves) now basked in the glory of God in heaven, blissfully relieved of their corporeal burden. The early Christians, to the great shock of their Roman oppressors, bravely stepped into the ring with hungry lions who predictably, and as if by design, always tore them apart and devoured their flesh. The diminishment of the material world—including the natural world—worked as a necessary corollary to the elevation of the spiritual.

And yet for the more apocalyptically minded Christians, I wondered if a desecrated body might present more disquiet. Technically, in End-Times theology, only the soul of the deceased rested in heaven with God—not the body—and only Jesus' Second Coming would raise the dead in their "resurrected and glorified bodies." To me, as to most believers, I presumed, the exact transaction remained pretty mysterious beyond the obvious image of grave doors flying open and millions of corpses clattering to heaven. Was it exclusively the dead body Jesus remade, or could he also conjure a new one?

I had two other thoughts about the families and their relationship to the dead. The first transcended religion and cut across all demographics. It was about the body itself. Some living bodies had been close to those once-living bodies. They were lovers, daughters, sons, fathers, and mothers of those bodies. They'd participated in the special human bond of touch, the intimacy of the social animal that made its indelible impression on our primate brains.

Now those bodies were dead and that was hard enough. And now they were separated from those bodies and that was harder still. But to think of their people as lost among the others at the Tri-State Crematory, in the myriad and awful fashions arranged by Brent Marsh, was a dark thing indeed. Such transgression affected humans terribly, changing them forever at their core.

Another phenomenon also dealt with how the victims thought about their own bodies. How racism had inscribed and scarred their own bodies. About half the desecrated corpses were white, roughly corresponding to the racial makeup of corpses received at Tri-State. Brent Marsh, it seems, was an equal opportunity desecrator. And yet it had to inflame racial passions for some white Southerners to discover—having entrusted their deceased relative to a white funeral home—that a black crematory operator had dishonored the body. It was sad to think that some people would almost certainly blame the entire race of the perpetrator.

The summer of 2002 passed in silence, with no further disclosures about Tri-State. Suddenly, in September we learned that a good percentage of the families could have been spared the trauma of the desecration.

Again, Norman Arey presented the news for the *Atlanta Journal-Constitution*, reporting that the Walker County Sheriff's Department had failed to act decisively on a tip about decomposing bodies at the Tri-State Crematory. And with this, a weirdly Gothic Southern tale came to life, filled with dark turns.

It all began on October 3, 2000—sixteen months before officials ultimately moved in—when a new propane delivery man, Gerald Cook, appeared at Tri-State for a routine service call. Having arrived before Brent Marsh, he began looking around the property for a large enough tank for his deposit. As he later stated in court, he observed a tremendous amount of "trash and debris . . . just clutter, a lot of junk. It was scattered everywhere." And when he turned the corner of one building, suddenly he saw skeletal remains—skulls, bones, and "one whole body with a little skin clinging to it" apparently heaped together by a nearby backhoe. Concerned and disturbed, Cook related the experience to his boss, who the next day reported the entire story to Sheriff Wilson.

Shockingly, the police did nothing. As Sheriff Wilson explained in the newspaper, "I felt it was a regulatory issue at the time . . . bodies not being disposed of in a timely manner. There wasn't much we could do then. If somebody tells me they saw bodies at a funeral home, I would expect that."

It seems odd, to say the least, that skulls and bones and skinless corpses piled high behind a building by a backhoe could be so easily dismissed. It is difficult to imagine, say, that one could legally dump bodies together in a mound at a funeral home and leave them outside for months. It would seem too that any understanding of decay—of skulls and bones versus freshly dead bodies—would mean that the bodies had been there a long time. And if the bodies had been there a long while, didn't that mean a family on the receiving end had been defrauded somehow? Personally I could think of an array of potential crimes suggested by the tip, some of which would ultimately prove untrue, from fraud to theft to organ trafficking. But even as he apparently assumed the tip to be valid—that bodies lay outside in a heap in various stages of decomposition—Sheriff Wilson stated it was "nothing to be upset about."

Which played into outsiders' black-humored comment that maybe folks up there in the Georgia hills were unfazed by bodies left out in the woods and junked together by a backhoe. Culturally, the joke went, it wasn't so much of a big deal. As a transplanted Southerner, I knew the joke wasn't quite fair. But in some ways I think the comedians were onto something. Maybe the old-line Protestant stranglehold on the culture, with its disavowal of this world while waiting for the next, rendered law enforcement peculiarly blasé to a report of torn and abused bodies lying decomposed in the open. In the Deep South, as the vision portends, nightmare rested just behind the eyes.

The tale went on.

By October 2001 the deliveryman, Gerald Cook, knew that the local authorities had no intention of investigating, having sat on the story for a year. And during that period he'd seen more compromised bodies, including one twenty feet from the propane tank so decomposed it appeared "like it was melted." This time he called his aunt, an administrative assistant for the FBI in Rossville, who anonymously contacted the Environmental Protection Agency. According to the newspaper account, when the EPA initially seemed skeptical about the story, she asked, "What if I told you I was walking my dog and the dog found a human bone, would that do?" Yes, that would do.

Now the EPA alerted the Walker County Sheriff's Department about a dog finding a human bone—the implication being that the dog had found the bone outside the crematory property. Federal pressure plus a dog and its bone. Finally the local police leapt into action.

So it was in November 2001—more than a year after the initial complaint—that Captain Stanfield knocked on Clara Marsh's door, located next to the crematory, and asked her about the dog and its bone. To this, Mrs. Marsh replied that the story just couldn't be true, and that her son, Brent, had traveled out of town. Stumped, Captain Stanfield returned to his car, and on the way looked around the buildings adjacent to Clara Marsh's house (noncrematory buildings) for human bones. He didn't see any. He then tried unsuccessfully to locate the dog but naturally could not find the complaining (and nonexistent) dog-owning neighbor. Having exhausted his leads, he reported back to his superior, Major Morrison.

As Major Morrison later correctly explained, Captain Stanfield couldn't search the crematory grounds without permission or a warrant. Quite incorrectly, though, Morrison stated, "We had no reason to suspect." Employing the same easy logic, they had strong reason to suspect: With two credible reports of decayed bodies, one from the propane deliverer and now another from the dog owner, they had solid grounds to "suspect" Brent Marsh of defrauding his customers. The time lag necessitated such a conclusion. All they had to do was present their credible evidence to a judge, who would have swiftly granted a search warrant for Tri-State based on "probable cause."

With two strikes against the Walker County Sheriff's Department, maybe the federal authorities were not willing to risk a third. After Gerald Cook's aunt again contacted the EPA in February 2002, this time more specifically detailing the horrible things her nephew had seen, the EPA sent its own people to the crematory. Outside a fence at Tri-State, these agents discovered a human skull, quickly bringing an end to Brent Marsh's secret career in modern-day alchemy.

But the damage was done. Ultimately the sheriff's department's apparent blunders, by my own estimation, allowed the desecration of up to a hundred additional bodies, as well as the problematic cremation of perhaps a hundred more. These were horrors perpetrated in this world, on this side of heaven and hell, on this side of the biblical Apocalypse.

22

UNFORTUNATELY FOR ME, and others, the biblical Apocalypse did not coincide with my own private apocalypse, the one I'd arrived at on the road.

Even for End-Timers, who believe in the literal fact of Revelation, the cataclysm remains an event of the future. The thousand-year reign of Christ on earth, the raising of the dead in their "glorified bodies," the founding of "a new heaven and a new earth"—all these longed-for events remain a few steps away.

My tribulation, on the other hand, unfolded in a brighter present. I traveled through my ruin, and the road went everywhere. And by now I realized that my portal no longer resembled a line of photographs hovering in the distance, a movable doorway in a remote region of sky. Instead, the entrance lay behind me in the form of revelatory messages nailed to wood just after the suburbs and dead ends of Tuscaloosa, the transparent flags straight from the Holy Ghost asking that I *Please do God's will today*. And I guess I was doing God's will, as best I could saddled with my dead-ender's burden of unbelief and my A gene–triggered hypersensitivity in which God's will had become our will and we had spoiled everything. Now I rode inside tribulation itself, headed inexorably toward a final freeze-frame.

Faster I sped back to Highway 69 and took off north-northeast through wooded hills scarred by tiny dirt roads leading up to timber clear-cuts; past black-eyed Susans in ditches, swaths of kudzu, an occasional farm; past the hamlet of Bremen and more of the same until I reached Dodge City—no Wild West town this place but a regular disturbed area complete with McDonald's, Conoco, Jack's, Dollar General, and Texaco—and then onto the entrance ramp at Interstate 65. It was my trip's sole stretch of superhighway and immediately I was struck by its smoothness—the extreme glassiness of surface like all those fake lakes I'd encountered, past and present, the mirroring effect on hungry eyes.

Again I rolled down my window, and the cars and trucks and world outside seemed farther away than usual—a trick of perspective, a streaming of events that had clear direction, yes, but no chance of balance or organization. Our world was like one of those old pinball machines I'd played as a kid, a zinging contraption we'd shoved so hard the TILT light came on and now the levers didn't work—but still, stupidly, we kept flapping away at the air, unaware the game was over and we'd lost our turn.

Stupid humans, I thought. Isn't that what each disciple admitted off camera? In their moments of letting go, didn't they ask forgiveness for being limited and stupid guys? Maybe we had to admit our own stupidity to understand the grandness of our self-inflicted debacle. And—following all manner of signs—I exited Interstate 65 at the town of Good Hope.

Historically speaking, I wasn't the only one who had a problem with apocalyptic ground.

> *. . . I looked and He opened the sixth seal, and behold, there was a great earthquake; and the sun became black as sackcloth of hair, and the moon became like blood . . .*

No, I don't mean those, not the five separate earthquakes mentioned in Revelation—but the three big ones that rattled out from the New Madrid fault from December 1811 to February 1812, still the greatest rumbles east of the Rockies since the European settlement. With a roar like thunder, the land surged and dropped, fissured and sank, blew sand into the air in small volcanoes, and ejected coal from black swamps. Along the Mississippi River, the uplifts created waterfalls and sent forth huge waves that gave the illusion the mighty river had changed direction, flowing backward to the north. Entire islands disappeared. A vast nonfake lake of twenty-five thousand acres formed in Tennessee, called Reelfoot Lake, as water from the river poured into a wide subsidence. Yet it wasn't merely the intensity of the quakes emanating from the bootheel of Missouri but the extraordinary breadth of the affected area: Sidewalks trembled in New York, buildings shook in D.C., church bells rang out in Boston.

And the quakes kept coming: Two hundred moderate-to-large tremors occurred through March and hundreds of small shudders continued into the next year. Day after day of unsteadiness, with each first tremble hinting at an ultimate rise and fall.

Such unprecedented shaking activated eschatological thoughts in many people, including the Cherokees, whose mountain homeland lay just a few hundred miles away. It was a rough time for the tribe: Americans continued their land incursions, the frontier market economy destabilized traditional roles, and Christian missionaries hammered away against their long-held spiritual practices. As a result, some Cherokees embraced the new ways and converted to Christianity, discarding their collectivized methods and creating larger and larger farms. A small percentage even went so far as to purchase black slaves to work those farms. In response to all this upheaval, the Cherokee apocalyptics— who tended to come from more traditionally minded people—cautioned the tribe that by abandoning the old ways they would suffer divine retribution. Following one quake in March 1812, a Cherokee conjurer, who may or may not have possessed the A gene, warned of "intense darkness" that would last three days, "during which all the white people would be snatched away as well as all Indians who had any clothing or household articles of the white man's kind." Some believed it was already too late. An old woman named Laughing Molly warned that "hailstones as large as hominy blocks would fall, all the cattle would die and soon thereafter the earth would come to an end."

Not to be left out of a good doomsday story about the South, de Soto passed somewhere near the bottom of the earthquake zone 270 years before the first tremor. Following a battle with the Pacaha Indians, which culminated in the desecration of a burial temple, the explorer sent scouts into the very heart of that precarious bootheel to look for treasure and a northwest passage to the sea. But the land appeared thinly populated, and so de Soto—whose marauding was not of the sustainable variety—couldn't travel in that direction without a proper concentration of Native settlements to pillage. Even if a land corridor to the water did exist, his army would starve trying to reach it.

And even worse, there was no gold. No silver. No rich and glorious civilization waited to the north, glinting in the sun. As far as booty was concerned, he was stuck with those crappy freshwater pearls he'd looted long ago.

With such bad news, the exalted commander must have begun to consider that after all the miles and everything his soldiers had endured—after all the arrows and spears they'd dodged and all the Indians they'd lanced from their tall horses—the expedition had simply failed.

A man like de Soto had only one choice. He told his soldiers to keep going. He pointed his army west and then south again, on what would become an increasingly disordered path.

By June 2003, after more than a year of official silence, we abruptly received new information about Tri-State from the deposition of the chief medical examiner of the state of Georgia.

Most startling to me, the medical examiner revealed that my father had been one of the earliest unfortunate arrivals at the site, one of only five identified bodies left uncremated during the initial year of 1997. Until the deposition, the greater public, including me, had no idea of the number of bodies abandoned each year, or that only five identified corpses had been desecrated in that beginning year. Apparently Brent Marsh accelerated his alchemical activities as time progressed. In addition to the five in 1997, authorities had managed to identify twenty-seven uncremated bodies for 1998, forty-three for 1999, forty-nine for 2000, eighty-one for 2001, and nineteen for 2002 (the story having broken in mid-February of that year).

With this revelation, my conception of my father's place in the desecration changed dramatically. In truth, I hadn't given the timing much consideration. For all I'd known, Brent Marsh had commenced his abandonment with good speed, having performed a number of dark tricks by

October 1997, the month my father appeared at Tri-State in his dirty coffin. As it turned out, the pits had yet to be dug and the burial vaults to be filled. The woods and out-buildings were not yet littered with corpses. Whatever it was that ultimately set Brent Marsh off, that triggering event had not occurred. If it was hoarding disease, it hadn't clicked in; if it was something else—something I couldn't even guess at—it hadn't happened.

As I digested the new numbers over the next several days, I realized it was quite possible that my father's was the first body abandoned at the site, having arrived in his en-closed casket after being underground those seven years. From the deposition it appeared that only a few bodies had shown up in caskets, and undoubtedly none of the others, given the infrequency of exhumation, had come from the ground.

Could my father have been the activating agent of the Tri-State story? Had Brent Marsh simply dragged his cof-fin off a little ways into the woods, a less pressing (and less putrefying) problem to be taken care of on the next day? Was my father the trigger?

Maybe one thing led to another—a body left here and a body tossed there, and so the great disturbance began. Surely he could get away with this one, the proprietor-alchemist must have thought, and he did get away with it for five years.

For me, this knowledge cast my father in quite a different role. He was not merely the familiar body whose death I experienced concretely on the ground, an expired thing who showed me what it was like being dead. Instead he was the first, or nearly the first, a lone sentinel whose tenure marked the entire span of the Tri-State Crematory Incident. Along with Brent Marsh, he was there from the beginning.

And he knew something else the others didn't know: what it was like being dead. In fact he'd been dead nearly seven years—a unique experience that provided a wealth of knowledge for the latest arrivals concerning their new state and their new home. He could reassure the newly dead—he could show them they were not alone. In my mind, he became the keeper and gatekeeper of the Tri-State Crematory, watching silently as Brent Marsh made his choices.

Mostly, they had either the vaults or the pits, either the flesh-reducing burial vaults or shallow trenches in the ground. As my father explained to these unlucky arrivals, they would endure the brunt of desecration, losing themselves into the bodies of others, DNA vanishing too quickly into the commingled darkness. For the more fortunate there were the woods, a scattering in the brush that allowed some individual change and a change of seasons. It was a better fate, my father explained, except for the animals and the elements, the coyotes and rain.

I took some odd comfort in this concept. My dead

father, as witness, recorded each body's placement at Tri-State. He drew a map of the grounds and numbered each discarded corpse, cross-referencing each number to his numbered list. It was some solace, I supposed, my father's Book of the Dead, though I imagined the book written in a language inaccessible to the living. Ultimately his evidence wouldn't help, for example, when the authorities rushed in on Brent Marsh's day of reckoning. Still someone kept track. The keeper kept track.

And my father revealed to all the new arrivals his own experience of being dead, delivering his soliloquy in the same unknown tongue. And though the story slipped away in that incomprehensible language, I knew his general theme, I knew the message I'd gleaned so far from playing dead. To be dead, my father taught—or, more accurately, his body taught—was about returning to the earth. Always dust to dust. It was an old story and the only story. Heaven lay in the ground.

The irony was not lost on me that I could feel my father more dead than alive.

After my graveside failure to imagine his dead body, I'd changed my approach. Having failed in one connection, I'd tried again. And so from the beginning, with both his exhumation and Tri-State, I'd made him a witness to his own decay and the loud deposit of bodies in the split ground. Denied my own ritual by desecration, I'd begotten a thing observant of the rituals of the dead; I'd begotten a father who so tangibly showed me his fading flesh that I learned to look out from his vacant eyes. I'd learned too well to consider the dead, causing my brain to backfire in the rawness of it all.

And though less intense than my father's gone body, the gatekeeper story felt closer to me than any pictures of my living father. Even the bad images, the one, for example, of the baseballs hurtling toward my head in our ugly backyard, felt clouded by resentment, a hazy anger occluding pieces of time I couldn't quite grab hold of. And the good ones, the ones I couldn't imagine at all, these lay even farther back from my border of sullenness.

But now the chasm offered a second chance. Not only might my father appear along the road like one of my wildflowers, sprung from disturbed ground, but I sensed another looming presence as well. All around the End pressed forward from the troubled background of Alabama, past and present, and from the troubled arc of my own history and those Tribulation images of the Tri-State Crematory. On this trip I rode with apocalypse. I rode inside. And certainly that terrible event, both real and figurative, felt more alive than my alive father. I could feel the burgeoning power of its linkage—the exhilarating mix, in the alchemical dark of my mind—of prophecy, father, Shit Fairy, photographs, suburbs, lakes, bodies, and the South. I could feel the blending of all these and more, a movement whose thrill felt a little like love.

And amid this sweep of convergence and acceleration, it seemed like time itself was coming to an end. A final scene in a final act. And yet wasn't this direction set in motion long ago, when my father snapped his first pictures of apocalypse? Hadn't he crunched our linear time together? The past flew toward us and entered our eyes; our eyes flew back toward the past. And on that last day Jesus did all the shooting, and when he finished—when the aperture of the earth opened and closed in that final moment—everything was still-life all over.

23

ACCORDING TO SAINT PAUL, the actual phenomenon of time is different as it approaches an end point. It contracts. It piles up on itself like a train wreck. Increasingly, events from the past take on a symbolic quality, and then those events come crashing into the present, loaded with meaning. I like to think of it this way: In the End everything feels like déjà vu.

"Déjà vu," I said aloud, pronouncing it like a good Alabamian for effect: "deja view." As I approached the bridge for Guntersville, which was a nexus for many of the historical elements I'd already contemplated, the town seemed like a good place to get it straight: In a line loomed Hernando de Soto, the Cherokees, and the Confederacy. Just ahead stretched a massive fake lake.

Halfway across the bridge I stopped the car and got out—feeling biblical and tall in my black boots—and when some redneck teenagers in a Dodge Ram rode by and yelled, "Faggot," I didn't yell back. I was concentrated down to the optic nerve.

I began with the smooth water that lay beneath me. I closed my eyes. And suddenly through the sky fell the glittered bodies of river things—mollusks, frogs, and fish—descended from heaven in backward rapture and dropped once again into the flowing water. I saw a dark cloud of passenger pigeons blacken the horizon, their bodies plunged downward with the roar of shotguns. Now Union artillery pounded the town—flashing soldiers and light, soldiers and flags—while peaceable keelboats, flatboats, and steamboats carried slaves in manacles, carried Cherokees west to the land of the dead. Footmen in chain mail. Horsemen in armor. Mastiffs tearing flesh on the nearby shore. I said "amen" and opened my eyes. I crossed the long bridge to the other side.

The town of Guntersville seemed strangely civilized. Expensive houses dotted the surrounding hills. A restaurant called La Strada apparently served high-end Italian food, and elegant antiques stores lined the main street. A couple of kids ate cones outside an old-fashioned ice cream parlor in the perfectly cool May air. A big marina floated lavish boats nearby. Actually, it reminded me a little of a New England town—quaint, but not scary quaint like I'd experienced in Jasper.

The near-drunken sensation of my crunch-time extravaganza reminded me of how I'd felt back in Jasper, when I pointed the viewer at my flag case and ended up with a dizzying confluence of reflected images commingling me, my father, the Confederacy, and America, not to mention the discerning eye of the camera itself. And yet that earlier ricocheting of mixed symbols and people had somehow managed to retain a balanced and relatively rational structure. A complicated but coherent mirror held up to the world. An astonishingly real realism.

Inside apocalypse things were very different. Nothing was particularly real, or even particular, for that matter. The agent of my apocalypse (my mind, I supposed) had stripped actual objects of most of their first essence. Apocalypse, for me, was an emptying out of this world. Flowers, churches, even ice-cream-slurping children—everything, it seemed, floated more and more in the service of an exclusive and final symbolism. And inside gazing out, I saw very little of the original referents to hold on to anymore, leaving nothing to make sense of except the pressing onward. In here I had direction and synchronicity (a kind of direction itself), but the hurtling toward the End and the crunching of time seemed wildly out of control, even as my own personal conjuring and crunching abilities appeared to strengthen. I wondered if my autonomy wasn't itself an illusion, a phantom operating inside the black hole of the End.

24

~~~

THE STATE HAD TO DO SOMETHING with all those unknown bodies.

The final accounting left 114 unidentified, 34 of which
would not yield retrievable DNA samples due to embalming and/or the commingling of flesh in Brent Marsh's pits
and burial vaults. The other 80 simply had no relative or
friend who stepped forward to claim them, their corpses
as lonely in death as they most likely existed in the last
days of life.

So, after refrigerating the bodies for a couple of years,
in March 2004 the state arranged for their permanent
burial in a donated plot at the Tennessee-Georgia Memorial Park in nearby Rossville, Georgia. Once again the
backhoe opened the red clay and lowered these well-
traveled bodies into their new burial vaults, placed end to
end in a fresh trench near the cemetery gate. The state provided each vault with a number and corresponding file in

the improbable event that someone would later identify a particular lost body, in which case the backhoe would again be summoned and the ground divided. In the mass grave the authorities buried 133 individual vaults—114 for the intact bodies and 19 more for a collection of miscellaneous bones.

I had trouble with these troubled dead. I had trouble because I couldn't really think about them in their new home, though I could so easily imagine them lounging and scattered at Tri-State. And I could think about the claimed dead and the living people who claimed them. I could think about these people because they had names. But the others, the lost dead—I couldn't think about them outside of Tri-State and my gatekeeper father. They remained abstracted, which I knew was wrong.

From a distance, then, I watched as the gatekeeper strode through the crematory grounds in his stinking cowboy boots, his name rubbing against bone. He told these oblivion-bound dead of their predicament and placement, as well as their final destination in another trench beneath a single memorializing monument. He did what he could, scrawling their names in his Book of the Dead. Now they would not be just a number—Jane or John Doe #23, for example—tucked away in the ground and in a coroner's cold case file. Now somewhere, someplace, a mark recorded more than an X, indecipherable as it was and lodged in a ledger filled neatly with the strangest of hieroglyphics.

———

In an effort to assuage my sin of unfeeling, and to augment the good deeds of the gatekeeper, I decided to undertake a similar role for a different set of forgotten dead. I'd strive to give names to my mysterious Cherokee ancestors who allegedly walked the Trail of Tears in 1838. I'd try to identify these people long hidden in history to soften my guilt about the unnamed dead in the present. It was both a biblical gesture—begat, begat, begat—and a strange attempt at transference in an alchemical time.

So I undertook the task with some diligence and honor.

I began the backward trek through time—online.

Backward I traveled through ancestral trees created by others working to assemble the past. Backward I traveled through the various Cherokee census rolls; the ragged U.S. and state censuses of the nineteenth century; local land, marriage, and burial records; slave rolls. The goal was to find a Cherokee woman named Missouri Dukes supposedly born during the tribe's western exodus, born on the short stretch of the trail that crossed into southern Missouri. According to family lore, it was the chance location of her birth that accounted for her spectacular name.

But I had more than just a name. I had a dramatic folktale.

My grandmother told of knowing her "beautiful" grandfather, who had long black hair and dressed "like an Indian." Strikingly, the man wore a single black eye patch.

As the story went, the eye patch resulted from an encounter with several other of my distant relatives, brothers who'd cornered my great-great-grandfather on a back road somewhere in Arkansas and gouged out his eye for marrying their white sister. They put out his eye because he was an Indian. It was a tale my grandmother, who died in 2003 at the age of ninety-six, adamantly maintained with precision.

Unfortunately, my research turned up only contrary news. Missouri Dukes, for example, did not arrive uncomfortably in Missouri while her mother traveled the Trail of Tears but instead was born to white parents in Arkansas in 1826, twelve years before that tragic event. This meant that my grandmother's grandfather, the one with the long black hair and telltale eye patch, was not part Indian unless his father was an Indian. I did find the marriage record of Missouri Dukes and a man named William H. Smith in 1842 in Lawrence, Arkansas, yet that document, in the line given for such information, failed to provide the husband's race.

So I worked hard to identify this William H. Smith, as he remained our only concrete link to the Cherokees. Again, I checked the rolls and censuses and birth and death records, but he wasn't there. He apparently wasn't born anywhere and he had no family history. He hadn't served in any military campaign and never owned land in Arkansas. Presumably, he'd died by 1850, because I found Missouri Dukes Smith remarried on the 1852 census. But that's all. I had a name but not a man.

I had a dead end.

But I did have a few things on my side.

I had someone without any apparent history, which fit the profile of a displaced Indian.

I had a common name, William Smith, a name someone might choose when trying to survive the onslaught of white culture, a name so common as to be plucked from thin air . . .

And I had my story, whose concrete details were so vivid and specific as to preclude conjuring. Who would make up such a tale? Why? And of course the violence of the tale seemed all too real and familiar—so ordinary as to be humanly true.

As I climbed higher into the hills beyond Guntersville, named after a half-Cherokee trader, I noticed I drove faster now and that objects beyond me continued to slip away from their normal consequence. Before, I had focused on the tiniest flowers lingering by the road. I had consulted my field guide. Now those same flowers seemed abstract, emptied of their original significance, as my call to apocalypse drew me farther away. And words—the normally reliable signs that provided our regular meaning—had become dislodged from their things.

It must have been the same, I thought, for Brent Marsh. For him, the bodies kept piling up in the present—year after year of corpses literally stacked on top of each other in pits and burial vaults. The bodies kept arriving from the past into the present and there was no more room. And as they piled up, day after day and month after month, they lost their regular meaning for him. They were not bodies with names to be cared for with ritual, bodies that once belonged to people. Rather, the names fell away as he stacked them higher. He, too, was looking past this world. The bodies with names became just things.

Tellingly, I passed a patch of orange-waving coneflowers, which just an hour before would have imprinted itself upon my brain, triggering my synapses into an indelibly brilliant photograph. But now they were just another in a series of distant images wallpapering the road: flowers, orange.

And lacking particularity, the things themselves appeared more two-dimensional than three, like those hand-painted signs—those admonitions—hanging on trees and posts outside Tuscaloosa. Maybe the names of things helped provide dimensionality, I thought, because now the whole landscape was flatter—hanging statically in the background like a car scene in an old movie, a blank screen upon which to project history and memory, the Cherokees whose former territory I traveled through, the unknown dead of Tri-State.

25

~~~

I DIDN'T THINK about what I'd planned as I drove my last hour to the Tri-State Crematory.

Not the Ridge and Valley that divided Alabama and Georgia—a thin strip of land forged from three different mountain-building episodes beginning half a billion years ago—three great heavings that folded and buckled the ground into consecutive waves of geology piling up against the old plateau to the west.

Not the deep shadows of the heavenly Appalachians—a range once thrust higher than the Himalayas by the tectonic collision of North America and Africa three hundred million years ago.

Not a quarter of a billion years of wind that blew shale and limestone into river valleys and left harder sandstone ridges stacked taller on both sides—valleys that later would become corridors for Native Americans to migrate along, always farther south into the land of animals, and for invading Europeans to enter the frontier and take that land away.

Instead, driving over Lookout Mountain into the last valley of the Tri-State Crematory, where my father once lounged in his casket of mud, I left a tape recorder switched on next to the flag case reflecting bright angles in the late-afternoon light. And soon I was just talking—talking to my recorder and then talking to air, talking to the South outside my window that really was not the South anymore but snatches of disconnected pictures, words, glimpses of words, the names of things floating by and repeated more or less indiscernibly, houses that were no longer houses and farms that were no longer farms, clicking images bleary as the photograph I had of the crematory grounds now lying half hidden on my car floor.

But from inside this view, my road was not a road and the wind was not wind. And my recorder was not a recorder but a doomsday machine, capturing small pieces of breath. And it told of words that had become just words, of sounds torn from the objects they once adorned . . . sounds, I thought later, resembling those of a demon or an angel but nothing in between.

It told of Highway 337 and the alchemy of drought . . . of the Shit Fairy and father flowers and peppergrass and mustard seed . . . of glorified goldlike bodies of bones.

It told of rats and snakes and vaults and limbs . . . of Noah floating on the fakest lake of all . . . of missiles and ghost lilies and a gatekeeper's eyes . . . of bomb shelters and boots and crosses and bars.

Not words I would later remember saying, or a

landscape I remembered passing, but tellings from the farthest edge of Babel—a flood of *deja view* saying kudzu and concrete, X's and flags . . . dead ends, de Soto, Cherokees and slaves . . . shutters and lenses and levers and clicks . . .

And finally, when I turned onto Center Point Road and passed the Center Point Baptist Church, the voice simply said I was there.

Through what I guessed was Brent Marsh's backyard, I glimpsed a black lake that quickly disappeared into leaves. A few hundred feet ahead lay the long crematory driveway. I snapped off my recorder and pulled over.

Already the sun had fallen below the ridge to the west and I heard the distinct hiss of a mockingbird in a tree. I felt the dirt and rocks through the thin soles of my boots and smelled a strong sweetness all around. To the south stretched my field. A fence hedge of honeysuckle, its white flowers overflowing above my head, forced me to step to the field's edge for a better view—led me to the exact position where the photographer of my ancient picture had once stood. Nearby a Southern dog wailed wildly in the woods. A clattering truck rolled by too slow.

The field I stared at now was mostly high grass, bluestem, I thought, with the two larger trees looming in the center. Gone were the tread marks of the bulldozer, the etched dirt that looked as scarred as the moon. Gone were the black-eyed Susan, Venus's looking glass, and sweet everlasting—those first flowers. Gone were the bodies locked in the earth or rotting on the ground. Gone were the bones except the shards of bones. Gone was my father's body stretched out in his coffin.

For a long time I waited in a low wind, listening to birds.

And once more I didn't think about what I'd expected to think after all those years. I didn't think about my father as first resident and gatekeeper, about Brent Marsh practicing his dark magic, about the bodies accumulating in woods, vaults, and pits. I didn't think about the fake lake I couldn't see that lay beyond the trees. Instead, in the last light of this particular day, my pilgrimage day, I had the weird idea that the whole place would burst into flowers—the whole expanse of my photograph would fill with leaf buds of every kind, every species from my field guide leaping from the page and blossoming in the half dark. Not fleabane and chickweed and thistle but a rush beyond saying, names beyond naming. They'd bloom and press and tangle inside the four corners of my vision—flowers for the dead and the bones of the dead, flowers for the living, flowers for time piling up on itself. And when that didn't happen—when the flowers didn't rise and fall back to earth—I guessed I was done. I guessed my journey was over.

I had to turn the car around, so I followed the dirt road to the left and arrived at what must have been the Marsh family church. There, in the bad light of the tiny graveyard, I could still make out the name of Brent Marsh's father on a headstone, planted only a quarter of a mile from where my own father had waited aboveground in his boots. Again I passed the dark field fallen back to grasses. No moon. I clicked one more photograph out my window and drove the short distance to the main road.

It was an undivided four-lane that led to Chattanooga, not much traffic, and I pointed the car northward and pulled to the side. It was finished, I thought. My father had not returned. And then suddenly I was crying and he was there in the car next to me, a shape, a presence, and I could feel him again as I had felt him as a young child. He was a vision—sprung from that flag case and from history, from the End and from the road. That's all I can say for sure. He was there for a while and I could feel him, real as a crush of flowers. He was close by and then he was gone.

Part Three

26

~~

THAT NIGHT I did what many Americans might do after a long day at the end of the world—I went to a convenience store and bought some beer. I rented a cut-rate hotel room in LaFayette and had a little wake for my thrice-dead dad.

In the traditional wake, the dead body lies present before the mourners who hold vigil through the dark hours. In my ritual, my father's image still shimmered brightly, so close it had not yet receded into the hold of memory. From the car I brought the cheap flag case, his mirrored portal.

It was clear that things had changed from that first stumble back in Tuscaloosa. Originally I traveled from here to there, from a place where I held only a photograph of a field to the actual three-dimensional field at Tri-State. A beginner, I'd embarked on a pilgrimage to an unholy place to acknowledge the dead. But apocalypse had intervened. Crunch time had arrived. And so my trip had become a pilgrimage to the End and all the overlay of biblical pronouncements that entailed. If the Apocalypse was already under way, asked my trip, didn't someone have to be my savior? After an Armageddon of fissuring words, didn't someone have to appear again who had appeared before? Eventually my father appeared, first intimated by a field of flowers and then as a presence breaking through the reflected glass of stars and stripes.

Given the tangle of figuring and prefiguring, I knew it would take a while to sort out what this personal revelation really meant. The connections were as interwoven as the blossoms in that bursting field. But I also knew, gazing at my beer—a red-white-and-blue can of Pabst Blue Ribbon—what I'd known from first flash: It had something to do with feeling. Or, more correctly, it involved the connection between saving and feeling. This evening I could suddenly feel my father again, hovering close by in that seat. He was not just a name or my father or a dead guy in boots but someone who was finally right there with me. Not a memory sensed through a veil of resentment, the way I'd experienced my father since adolescence, but a creation transported by crunch time into all my father ever was, a presence who had delivered me from unfeeling, from a life without my father except an abstract father.

All of which led back to apocalypse—my father and the world being so entwined. Maybe there was a new kind of End-Times living that would not draw me away from this world but would bring me back here. Not empty it out, as had long been my inclination, but create a change of direction that would focus my vision on this place and blue-shift things here. Find the countervailing force to all that dark energy.

As I finished my first beer and opened the second, I noticed that the red bar, which lay behind a blue seal with the beer's name, resembled half of the X on the Alabama state flag (the same X that itself stood for the X on the Confederate Battle Flag). Understandably, I hadn't considered this in consuming a thousand other PBRs. And below these emblems stretched a wreath of barley and hops, cultivated remnants of wildflowers . . . Smiling, I couldn't help but consider the link to Revelation as well as the disparity of my situation, how instead of divining the seven seals from heaven, I was reduced to reading the seals of beer cans in a lousy hotel . . .

And bereft as I was of any religious salvation, however much I longed for the clarity of that telling and saying, I mouthed the words to Depeche Mode's "Personal Jesus"—hearing, instead of the '80s English band's rendition, the low voice of Johnny Cash in one of his last recordings: "Flesh and bone by the telephone / Lift up the receiver / I'll make you a believer." Was this my last chance? I picked up the landline from the night table but no one spoke back.

And then after my third and final beer, I had this thought—his body fading to slow fires—I thought now, in conjuring his presence over time, maybe I'd learn to love my father again. That was my revelation, and like the best biblical one it was mostly about love.

I scoured my can for any additional alchemical message—like the secret to the elixir of youth, of immortality—but none appeared. I put down the empty vessel and went to bed.

27

~~~

THE TRI-STATE CREMATORY INCIDENT would also come
to a close. Judgment Day would arrive for Brent Marsh.

First the civil case rolled around in March 2004, incit-
ing a media extravaganza. Would Brent Marsh testify,
revealing something we didn't know about his motivations, some key to his bizarre actions?

As it turned out, every important pretrial decision went
against the defendants. (The defendants in the civil case
were the Tri-State Crematory and a number of local funeral
homes that had used the crematory's "services" through
the years.) The judge allowed testimony from victim family members regarding emotional distress and, most sig-
nificantly, ruled that jurors could view photographs of the
decayed and discarded bodies.

Imagine a juror seeing a slide show presentation featuring my father's twelve-years-gone body laid out in his
coffin, the melted flesh of a mass grave, and the "reduced"
corpses of a burial vault.

The defendants didn't have a chance.

And encountering such inflammatory evidence, they settled, resulting in no new information entered into the record and no testimony by Brent Marsh.

So our last opportunity resided with the criminal case against Brent Marsh, which finally reached the court docket in November 2004. It was a massive indictment, charging him with 122 counts of burial fraud, 47 counts of giving false statements, 179 counts of abuse of a dead body, and 439 counts of theft by taking. Again we all hoped that Brent Marsh would testify, as would an array of criminologists and psychologists. Soon the public record would be filled with information that would illuminate and clarify his motivations.

But this was not to be. Faced with the strong possibility of several decades behind bars, Brent Marsh pled guilty on all counts of the indictment. He never took the stand. No public record of any interest developed in the case—the judge ordered no psychological evaluations, and no expert witnesses took the stand. It was as if the alchemist had cast one last veil of smoke over the entire proceedings.

Yet we did finally hear from Brent Marsh. As part of his plea bargain—in which he was sentenced to twelve years in prison—he was required to write a letter of apology to each victim's family. It included the following lines:

As I have stated in court, I have not the answers that you so greatly desire. I wish I had the answers to give you ease, but I do not. Therefore, I can only offer you my deepest apology.

It was a handwritten form letter, composed as if by a machine, the style somehow robotic. It contained the correct condolences and the words were true: On some level it seemed obvious that Brent Marsh had no conscious idea why he'd desecrated hundreds of bodies, which confirmed my original conclusion. I had always suspected no greater plan lay behind his deceit.

In reading the letter, however, for the first time I experienced the identity of our names as a hard jolt. Certainly I'd considered the irony before, but I'd never really felt it viscerally. I saw "Brent" signed at the bottom of the page, and its inescapable connection to my name, my life, rushed forward. Suddenly the old letters were inscribed in a new way upon my brain.

From that point on, my regular name floated on a smooth surface and, when I heard it or read it somewhere, the other Brent would always dart beneath that plane. It was not a conscious phenomenon, just as Brent Marsh's actions were not self-evident to him, but more of a synaptic subfiring that I could never quite get rid of. It seemed that Brent Marsh traveled with me through this world, a brother of sorts who shared my name.

And when I did think more concretely about our collective identity, it typically was not in the present but in the past. When Brent Marsh's father called for his child across the lake—perhaps to help with the incineration of a corpse or to flip the oven's switch—he called my name, too. And when my own father called for me across the suburban backyards pocked with bomb shelters, he likewise summoned his persecutor in death. On the one hand it wasn't a big deal; I didn't dwell on the connection in a particularly obsessive way. On the other hand it was always there, an imprinted guilt by association that lurked deeper down.

Even more strange regarding the letter, Brent Marsh got my father's name wrong: "I am very sorry for your loss of the late Mr. Robert Hendricks." His name was *Ronald*, not Robert!

How was that possible? Why my letter of all the hundreds he had to write? Did the Shit Fairy suddenly alight atop his pen, curving different symbols across the page?

After everything having to do with names—from my father's boots to the gatekeeper's book—what were the chances Brent Marsh would make such an error?

And beyond the personal coincidences, the misnaming conjured images of the unknown dead of Tri-State, those unfortunate souls who lay alongside one another in a row of graves with one memorial marker in Rossville, Georgia. Their names would never again be attached to them upon this earth. And it was all because of Brent Marsh, whose cleaving of bodies and words—of looking beyond this world toward somewhere else—left a large swath of disturbance just behind him.

De Soto spent the last year of his life—the year after passing through the lower edge of the New Madrid earthquake zone—wandering around what is now Arkansas. With his best translator having perished, he had difficulty gaining accurate information from his Native captives, no matter how much he tortured them. In more ceremonious exchanges, he had a hard time understanding the various chiefs. And given the new language divide, he therefore had trouble planning his next move—first swerving toward Oklahoma and then veering back down to the Mississippi River.

By April 1542, he'd reached the eastern side of the big river, not too far from the steamboats of modern Natchez, and set up camp in a conquered town. This time he sent his emissaries south, on the chance they'd find treasure but more immediately to locate an overland route to the Gulf of Mexico. A week later he learned the bad news: no gold and no path.

De Soto was in trouble. Having lost three hundred of approximately seven hundred men—and, more significant, 150 or so of his original 200 horses—he desperately needed to resupply. Those all-important horses, for example, had not received new iron shoes for over a year.

Now, if he wanted to exit this increasingly hostile scene, he'd have to construct a small armada of seaworthy boats, and if he ever managed to arrive home, he'd have to explain himself to his investors and to the king.

As the esteemed historian Charles Hudson suggests, "This realization must have been almost a physical blow to De Soto"—the once indomitable conquistador soon "became ill and took to his bed, no doubt depressed." But I'm pretty sure it was the Shit Fairy, and the Shit Fairy was a long way from being done.

When de Soto died a few weeks later, his handpicked successor ordered the body hidden for three days and then buried, at night, so as to perpetuate the ruse of the man's divinity. Though we have no evidence that the local Indians believed in de Soto's holy powers, despite his many tricks with mirrors, perhaps his followers were willing to make the extra effort at concealment under the circumstances.

The threat of desecration also existed as a real possibility. If the Native people knew where to look, they might later dig de Soto up, slice him into parts, and then dangle some choice pieces from trees. The soldiers had witnessed this spectacle visited upon several of their comrades. And though they themselves had cut off untold numbers of hands and noses—an act of terror performed on the living just to show they meant business—de Soto's fighters still couldn't abide the prospect of their leader's flesh becoming bird food. So they galloped their horses back and forth over the unmarked grave, as if in celebration of some saintly festival, to further deceive the onlookers.

Fearing that the deception had failed, however, the Spaniards themselves dug up the body, added sand to de Soto's winding sheets, and then re-interred him in a hollowed-out oak. They nailed a makeshift door over his face and towed the tree to the deepest trench of the Mississippi River. There, in the darkness, they sank him to the bottom. I wish I could say I could feel his body down there, the bones that may long ago have broken apart and that shifted and fell when the big earthquakes hit centuries later. But I can't. I can't feel anything about him. His body still lies there underwater—unidentified by human marker.

28

〰

A HOST OF ANGELS crowded at the base of the arched monument. They looked ceramic, or maybe plastic, although I was too afraid to touch them to make sure. One clasped her upraised palms together, and her blue dress appeared homemade, like a doll's dress with tiny beads. Another was painted and her hands were outstretched, deep folds flowing through her windblown blond hair and gown. A third angel, which looked suspiciously like a red Christmas tree ornament, played a dirty violin.

At first glance only the open greenness on all sides suggested that the granite monument marked something other than a single grave site. Sandblasted Gothic letters told the rest of the story.

GARDEN OF PEACE

This section of Tennessee-Georgia Memorial Park
is dedicated to those loved ones who were discovered at Tri-State Crematory on February 15, 2002
and laid to rest in, March 2004. May they and their
families have everlasting peace and consolation.

On the hillside of the large cemetery, roses and lilies lay
bunched and scattered beneath headstones. Carnations
and gladiolus glowed upon the graves. And below I could
see the unknown dead huddled in the depths where everything was black, including the iron-red dirt. I could see
the bodies lined up in a row, bones shifting only occasionally with the tectonic rumblings of the Ridge and Valley.

I sat down on the grass and pulled at the dirt.

I knew I'd never come here again.

And I wanted to give these dead a few roadside flowers
as a final offering, a pretty link to their last entry in the
historical record. But I'd come empty-handed. Instead I
fumbled in my back pocket for a frayed map of Georgia
and laid it next to the red angel. Now if Jesus happened to
summon these unclaimed dead on a fateful day—blowing
the doors off their matching vaults—they'd know the
name of the ground they rose from. And if he didn't, well,
at least someone had told them they were still in Georgia,
resting on a big hill called Missionary Ridge.

When I stood to go, the midmorning light had blanched

the headstones mostly white, and they seemed to float in air against the slope of the hill. I thought they resembled the little flags of apocalypse I'd seen outside Tuscaloosa the day before: white sheets of copy paper nailed to pines and oaks. These gentle admonitions had asked that I *Please do God's will today* and *Please do God's work as he wants you to.*

Earlier I'd wondered what my own sheets hammered to wood might say, whether they'd always remain blank or whether they'd display the blurred image of the Tri-State field I carried with me in my car. I'd hoped the grail of disturbed ground would adorn my flags.

And then I knew what I'd have on my sheets. It was the first ritual of coming home—of making the darkness visible and pulling my eyes back here.

In black letters I'd have just names—pages of single entries torn from my Book of the Dead and fluttering in whatever wind there was. The flags that harkened the close of this world for me were just words, little head-stones marking more doom. In a moment I imagined but did not see the whole Ridge and Valley papered with names, collapsing time as they glittered in light. In a land with no future every name should rise. And in my last act of rapture, suggesting nothing but the End, the ghosts gleamed all around me in that lush place full of trees.

Epilogue

AFTER THE EXHORTATION FOR THE MESSIAH to "come quickly," after the last "amen," the King James Bible concludes with the words THE END.

Followed by a period.

But my version of the King James Bible continues on long after that period. In the Topical Reference Bible that I own, a number of educational tools follow Revelation, the last chapter, including Comprehensive Bible Helps; the Whole Bible Arranged in Subjects; Alphabetical Index of Subjects; and finally, that most obsessive of scholarly endeavors, Cruden's Concordance to the Bible. And the continuation occurs because at the close of Revelation, the vision of apocalypse remains just that: a dream, a hallucination.

Therefore—even for someone with the A gene, for whom the beginning of the End had already commenced—I still felt some space for commentary, for further education and illumination. I decided to tie up smaller, less all-encompassing ends. The most important of these was to meet with Greg Ramey, the agent in charge of Tri-State for the Georgia Bureau of Investigation.

By the time I caught up with him on a cold fall day years after the case was closed, he worked out of an unmarked office near Rome, in what appeared to be an abandoned storefront in an isolated strip mall. A tough guy but kind, wearing his heavy gun with a natural grace, he showed a genuine interest in my inquiry and asked how my family—especially my mother—had dealt with the desecration. Also, in an effect both comforting and dislocating, he kept calling my father's body "your dad." He said we found "your dad" just a little ways into the woods, we found "your dad" after that first week, we found "your dad" in his casket. And without prodding he quickly laid out a clear picture of the crematory grounds and outbuildings, adding to the landscape I'd carried around so long in my head. He was, moreover, from the northwest corner of Georgia himself and was acquainted with all the actors in this backwoods morality play. He even knew about my father, he said. He had a few things for me.

My father's file was first. He handed it over. "Take as long as you'd like," he said, returning to the paperwork strewn across his desk.

As I paged through, I read that my dad was "mummified" and "partially skeletalized"—not surprising, I supposed, but it was different to see the words written down, different to think of someone standing over his rotten body, taking notes. I read that my father's teeth were in "good repair." I saw the word "possibly" scribbled next to a box checked "Caucasoid." And in a stark declaration as to the extent of decay, I found the "indeterminate" box checked rather than the "male" or "female."

With chart after chart itemizing bones and skin and hair, I began to feel disembodied as I sat in Agent Ramey's office or, more accurately, I began to feel the pull of my father's wasted body drawing me away from myself.

It was a relief, then, when I finally turned to the more familiar territory of the "Recovered Clothing Form." There I found a detailed description of my father's plaid shirt, brown jacket, Eddie Bauer chinos, Hanes briefs, and, of course, his custom-made cowboy boots. I must have mentioned something aloud about the boots, because Agent Ramey said he had a story about them. He gave me a small plastic bag, which I held up to the light.

My father's name floated before me—"**Ron Hend**ricks"—with the last letters more faded than the first. Instinctively I lifted the bag farther from my eyes. Cut into two pieces, the tan leather barely looked worn and the stitching barely frayed. It was a miracle, I thought, considering the burial and abandonment, a miracle my father's bootheel still offered its letters.

The other leather scrap had some writing, too:

Handmade By
Gallegos-Mendez

Santa Fe., N. Mex.
10188943-10
B10

The B10, I guessed, was my father's boot size, as he had unusually narrow feet (B) and always had trouble finding a comfortable fit. But I couldn't decipher the longer code above, probably a serial number of some sort with his size after the dash. The thought crossed my mind that the number had some incantatory purpose tied to the long life and preservation of leather. The quality of both cowhide and letters lent itself to such magical thinking.

"Go ahead and open it," Ramey said, meaning the bag. I did. I held my father's old bootheel in my hand, the piece with his name. In the open air the leather felt brittle, like a communion wafer, hard and dry. As the act wasn't something I'd ever contemplated, I didn't know what to do. I just kept turning the piece over and over in my hand. After a while it was too much, really, the weight of it all, so I put the bootheel back in its sleeve and listened to Agent Ramey's story.

As it happened, his experience in leading the Tri-State investigation had made him something of a celebrity in mass-crime circles. He was asked to give presentations to law enforcement groups and forensic specialists. The Tri-State crime scene, with its hundreds of bodies desecrated over time, presented different challenges from, say, an airplane crash with immediate carnage. And so, in developing his presentation, Agent Ramey prominently featured my father's body—"your dad" as he kept saying—and the story of the boots. In fact, he'd created a slide show that pictured not only my father's body in his grave clothes but also close-ups of the bootheel. He said the one with my father's name always brought down the house.

Understandably, I noticed the coincidence that my father, the consummate amateur photographer, had himself become the star of a traveling slide show in death. But I didn't have much time to dwell on that—or consider its connection to my apocalyptic envisionings—as Agent Ramey asked if I wanted copies of the photographs. He explained that some were pretty graphic. He said it was up to me.

In the end, I turned down the ones that showed my father's face. I couldn't do it. After all those years of imagining him dead, and of gazing at death from inside his eyes, I couldn't look into his dark sockets. Nightmare, I knew, lay just behind that stare. Any glimpse by me might stir the thing awake. I was relieved, then, when Agent Ramey advised against it, too.

In the photograph I did take from him, my father's skull lies outside the frame, and the rest of his body sprawls top to bottom. The grave clothes have all taken on a sepia tone against a white sheet, and the individual components—pants, shirt, jacket—look blended together in the loose fit and deep folds of a mythical range rider. His bare hand is recognizable to me, the curve of fingers and harmony of bone. The size and shape of the wrist looks right. In fact the whole line of his body seems familiar, imprinted in memory by a child's long study of form and detail. I thought how different this was from the last time I saw him alive, barely breathing in that high hospital room, when he didn't look like my father at all. How I couldn't feel anything as his body descended into the dark hole, a mound of dirt piled up nearby. Now I could sense his approach across the years. I wasn't afraid.

And there's a fluidity to the image as if the wind is blowing, blowing straight and hard from an unknown direction, until at the bottom of the photograph my father's socks protrude—enlarged by perspective and stiff as concrete. The most compelling piece of evidence lies draped across his legs. Cutting a diagonal that divides movement and stillness, arranged for documentation, rest those beautiful boots.

Yet even with this, Agent Ramey's performance wasn't over. At every juncture, he remained calm and steadying. He allowed me to collect myself. When he rose and walked into the next room, filled with computers and equipment, I followed.

The climax would be a video.

Again, he kindly inquired if I wanted to participate. "Sure you're ready for this?" he asked.

The video, he said, showed the nighttime raid on the crematory, in which a stunned Brent Marsh leads GBI agents through one of the buildings. I'm not sure which one, probably the large metal storage shed. It's dark inside, and the agents are using high-beam flashlights. And for the first time I hear Brent Marsh's voice—deep and soft. He's trying to explain why there are bodies lying all over the floor, trying to help the agents identify them. Maybe he's thinking if he can tell their names, then he might be okay. He might get away with it. Or maybe he's actually trying to help out—it's hard to say. There's an old woman's decaying body in the corner and some discussion about who she is. He fumbles with a ledger—like the gatekeeper, I thought—but it's pretty clear he doesn't know. After a while, he just goes quiet. His face is never shown.

Of all my experiences with Agent Ramey, the video remains most entwined with my dreams, my waking dreams of Tri-State. But my brain was pretty shot. After scanning my father's file and holding his bootheel, after tracing his hand and heavy socks, the images onscreen began to blur. Soon, I asked Agent Ramey just to turn the machine off. I thanked him and said goodbye.

Outside the wind was blowing. I didn't have a coat, and I shivered. Half an hour north lay Tri-State and a few minutes north of that sprawled the Chickamauga National Military Park—site of the last major Confederate victory of the Civil War. For a moment I thought of stopping by the park, of taking the driving tour through the stone monuments and regiment markers where thousands had fallen not so long ago, where pieces of bone lay locked in the ground. But it seemed too late for all that.

I started the car, turned on the heat. A blast of cold air blew across my face.

With a little luck, my flag and I might make it home before evening.

Acknowledgments

~~~

In addition to the *Original King James Version of the Bible* (Dugan, 1984), as well as *The HarperCollins Study Bible*, revised edition (New York: HarperCollins, 2006), the following books were indispensable in writing about my experiences: Giorgio Agamben's *The Time That Remains: A Commentary on the Letter to the Romans*, translated by Patricia Dailey (Stanford, CA: Stanford University Press, 2005) (Agamben makes the following translation of 1 Corinthians 7: 29–31: *But this I say brethren, time contracted itself . . . For passing away is the figure of this world*; he also links photography with apocalypse in his short essay "Judgment Day" from *Profanations*, translated by Jeff Fort [New York: Zone, 2007], a connection I seem to have arrived at independently); Gilles Deleuze's *Spinoza: A Practical Philosophy*, translated by Robert Hurley (San Francisco: City Lights Books, 1988); Charles Hudson's *Knights of Spain, Warriors of the Sun: Hernando de Soto and the South's Ancient Chiefdoms* (Athens: University of Georgia Press,

1997); Bart D. Ehrman's *Jesus: Apocalyptic Prophet of the New Millennium* (New York: Oxford University Press, 1999); Bertram Wyatt-Brown's *Southern Honor: Ethics and Behavior in the Old South*, 25th anniversary edition (New York: Oxford University Press, 2007); William G. McLoughlin's *Cherokees and Missionaries, 1789–1839* (Norman: University of Oklahoma Press, 1995); Stephen Sizer's *Christian Zionism: Road-map to Armageddon?* (Downer's Grove, IL: IVP Academic, 2004); Stephen Mitchell's *The Selected Poetry of Rainer Maria Rilke* (New York: Vintage, 1989); John M. Coski's *The Confederate Battle Flag: America's Most Embattled Emblem* (Cambridge, MA: Harvard University Press, 2005); and Dawnie Wolfe Steadman, Kris Sperry, Frederick Snow, Laura Fulginiti, and Emily Craig's chapter, "Anthropological Investigations of the Tri-State Crematorium Incident" in Bradley J. Adams and John E. Byrd, eds., *Recovery, Analysis, and Identification of Commingled Human Remains* (New York: Humana Press, 2008) (it is this scholarly article, written by the forensic investigators at Tri-State years after the incident, that provides the final number of desecrated bodies at Tri-State as 339 rather than 334, the total sometimes named in earlier newspaper accounts; the article also places the number of unidentified bodies at 114 rather than the earlier reported figure of 108).

Equally indispensable was the *Atlanta Journal-Constitution*, the newspaper I grew up reading. I thank it and particularly Norman Arey for his brilliant reporting on the Tri-State Crematory Incident.

I also personally thank Agent Greg Ramey of the Georgia Bureau of Investigation. In his forthcoming approach to the available information, Agent Ramey showed himself to be a kind and honorable public servant.

Donna Tartt, a native Mississippian, helped me navigate some of the regional issues in an early version of the book, and her editorial work proved invaluable. Thank you, Donna. And thank you, Joy Williams and Kathryn Davis, for being such generous spirits.

My appreciation also goes out to my agent, Zoë Pagnamenta, whose unflagging efforts carried the project to fruition. And I am forever indebted to my terrific editors at FSG—Paul Elie, Sean McDonald, and Emily Bell—as well as the many others there who labored to bring the book forward.

Much gratitude to my mother and sister for their understanding and for the hard work in putting together our collective history. And finally, I thank my daughter, Xia, who reminds me daily what it's like to be a kid, and my wife, Kate Bernheimer, who sustains me with her faith and love.